Mother of the Redeemer

ANNIVERSARY EDITION

POPE JOHN PAUL II

With Commentary by M. Jean Frisk

Pauline
BOOKS & MEDIA
Boston

Library of Congress Cataloging-in-Publication Data

Catholic Church. Pope (1978-2005 : John Paul II)

[Redemptoris Mater. English]

Mother of the Redeemer / Pope John Paul II ; with commentary by M. Jean Frisk. -- Anniversary ed.

p. cm.

Includes bibliographical references.

ISBN-10: 0-8198-4902-1

ISBN-13: 978-0-8198-4902-1

1. Mary, Blessed Virgin, Saint--Theology. 2. Catholic Church--Doctrines. I. John Paul II, Pope, 1920-2005. II. Frisk, M. Jean. III. Title.

BT613.C3513 2012

232.91--dc23

2012008058

Cover design by Rosana Usselmann

Cover art: Sassoferrato (1609–85) Madonna and the Child Jesus

Published by Pauline Books & Media, 50 Saint Pauls Avenue, Boston, MA 02130-3491

Printed in the U.S.A.

www.pauline.org

Pauline Books & Media is the publishing house of the Daughters of St. Paul, an international congregation of women religious serving the Church with the communications media.

1 2 3 4 5 6 7 8 9   16 15 14 13 12

Contents

�֍ �֍ ✦

Part I

Part II

Preface

Twenty-five years later, I find myself rereading a letter from a shepherd to his beloved!

Were his words read, remembered, heeded?

How were the Church and the lives of its members influenced by this letter?

Obviously, openly, John Paul II loved Mary—Mother of his people, protector, personal, intimate, confidant—who was and is actively present among us, and who had a significant role in salvation history. The wall outside his Vatican window was graced with her image, a crowned Mary, a gentle, sweet, western image of Mary. But no matter when or how she is presented to us, it's never Mary without her Divine Son!

When you love the shepherd, you tend to want to love who and what the shepherd loves. This letter awakened the curious and resonated in some corners.

During the leadership of John Paul II, seldom did he publish a writing, have an audience, or visit a country without specifically honoring the Mother of God—even if simply using a closing *pro forma* statement. Study of those apparently routine closings shows trends or issues dear to his heart at the time—not in the sense of an emotional endearment, but of a conscious point of reference for an educational goal as if to say: "Think about this!" So, what sort of legacy did Pope John Paul II leave with this particular document: *Redemptoris Mater*? Who read it? Who listened?

The document was published on the feast of the Annunciation, March 25, 1987, to announce the long-term preparation for the turning millennium. The Redeemer's 2000th birthday, born among us of a woman who freely accepted him, would begin with a year dedicated to his mother, to her birth, even if unknown in the annals of history. We were asked to study Mary's faith, to look at her role, and to imitate her.

Benedict XVI, John Paul's successor, adds an even stronger note when he directs the attention back to us. Her giftedness was not for Jesus alone, but also for us, just as our gifts are meant for one another. Benedict expresses it this way:

> Mary's birth constitutes a fundamental stage for the Family of Nazareth, cradle of our redemption, an event that regards each one of us, because every gift that God has granted to her, the Mother, he has granted thinking also of each one of us, her children.[*]

One year after *Redemptoris Mater* was published, the Vatican's Congregation for Catholic Education published *The Virgin Mary in Intellectual and Spiritual Formation*. In terms of research and teaching, this document analyzed *Lumen Gentium's* chapter 8 (the longest official Marian document

---

[*] Benedict XVI, Angelus Address at the Shrine of Bonaria in Cagliari, Sardinia, September 7, 2008.

ever published by a Council of the Catholic Church) and the post-conciliar documents focused on Mary,[**] specifically *Redemptoris Mater.* Clearly, the Congregation tried to implement a follow-up. It insisted on the *necessity* of furnishing seminarians and students of all centers of ecclesiastical studies with Mariological formation that embraces study, devotion, and lifestyle. These teachers of theology were now required to study about Mary, her person, and her active role in salvation history. They are to teach the faithful these truths. Honoring Mary's place as inseparable from Christ's Incarnation was to be considered essential to Church teaching. This was not to be left to personal choice, devotion, or interest. Learning about Mary's person and role is required. Teachers must exhibit the following qualities:

a. A *complete and exact knowledge* of the doctrine of the Church about the Virgin Mary, which enables them to distinguish between true and false devotion, and to distinguish authentic doctrine from its deformations arising from excess or neglect, and, above all, which discloses to them the way to understand and to contemplate the supreme beauty of the glorious Mother of Christ

b. An *authentic love* for the Mother of the Savior and Mother of mankind, which expresses itself in genuine forms of devotion and is led to "the imitation of her virtues" (LG, 67), above all to a decisive commitment to live according to the commandments of God and to do his will (cf. Mt 7:21; Jn 15:14).

[**] See especially, Paul VI, *Signum Magnum* and *Marialis Cultus.*

    c. The *capacity to communicate* such love to the Christian people through speech, writing, and example, so that their Marian piety may be promoted and cultivated.[†]

Did this happen? Admittedly, many of us are averse to the word must. *Must* study? *Must* love? *Must* communicate? What harried and over-extended bishop, priest, or layperson has time to do more than quickly scan so much written material?

Nonetheless, we do find traces, expressions, and ways of thinking that have their roots in the hearts of outstanding leaders who loved Mary. We remember the quiet work of those who prepared the draft of *Lumen Gentium's* chapter 8, a summation of years of studied wisdom, underscored by the studies from the French Mariological Society with the desire to see Mary deeply linked with the liturgy. Chapter 8 presents Mary as the summation of what it means to be a Church fully centered on Christ.

Then in the face of apparent controversies, Paul VI courageously gave Mary the title "Mother of the Church." We need to keep in mind that bishops the world over did not dismiss Mary's importance at the council. The questions debated about her largely centered on two points of view: Mary is exalted, precious, and important. Shouldn't she be worthy of her own specific document acknowledging this? The other perspective asked us to see her as a member of the Church, one of us, on our level, an example of who we should be. The vote won out

---

[†] This translation taken from *Mother of Christ, Mother of the Church: Document on the Blessed Virgin Mary* (Boston: Pauline Books & Media, 2001), 356.

for the second choice. For the Pope to then give her yet another title of honor among so many others, he was essentially saying: "Yes, she is truly one of us and our example, but she is also our mother with a mother's duty and right to continue caring for us and educating us—a mother who never forgets us and walks with us—her children—on our journey." As John Paul II tells us in regard to Mary's role in the Church: "Knowledge of the true Catholic doctrine regarding the Blessed Virgin Mary will always be a key to the exact understanding of the mystery of Christ and of the Church. . . . [I]n her new motherhood in the Spirit, Mary embraces each and every one *in* the Church, and embraces each and every one *through* the Church. In this sense Mary, Mother of the Church, is also the Church's model."‡

Today we are familiar with terms used in the encyclical, like Mary's active presence, Mary as Christ's first follower, his *first* disciple, Mary our forerunner and sister in faith, Mary's place in the Communion of Saints. But, perhaps one of the most subtle influences has to do with ecumenism. Through *Redemptoris Mater* we were challenged to think about Mary in ways we could imitate in our daily lives. At the time, these were new ideas for the lay faithful.

Admittedly in pre-Vatican II times, for various reasons including fear of losing authenticity and identity, the Catholic Church seldom spoke in genuine ecumenical terms—at least for the people in the pews. The Polish pope, John Paul II, shared the longing of John XIII who heeded the Spirit's

---

‡ See p. 86.

gentle call to look East and seek commonalities—to see Mary as love's conduit of unity.

Today, we dare to dialogue. We look at Eastern rituals and art with growing respect, and we are not afraid to learn of differences that can enrich, not endanger, our steadfast common faith in the Redeemer, Jesus Christ. Ecumenism for John Paul II meant "that *in the presence of the Mother of Christ we feel that we are true brothers and sisters* within that messianic People, which is called to be the one family of God on earth (50)."[*]

Accept this invitation to read or re-read, to ponder, to pray, and to act in the light of Blessed John Paul II's holy wisdom.

---

[*] Ibid, 308.

Topical Outline

Mother of the Redeemer

Redemptoris Mater

PROMULGATED BY
HIS HOLINESS POPE JOHN PAUL II

On March 25, 1987
On the Blessed Virgin Mary
in the Life of the Pilgrim Church

Venerable Brothers and dear Sons and Daughters,
Health and the Apostolic Blessing!

Introduction

1. The Mother of the Redeemer has a precise place in the plan of salvation, for "when the time had fully come, God sent forth his Son, born of woman, born under the law, to redeem those who were under the law, so that we might receive adoption as sons. And because you are sons, God has sent the Spirit of his Son into our hearts, crying, 'Abba! Father!'" (Gal 4:4–6).

With these words of the Apostle Paul, which the Second Vatican Council takes up at the beginning of its treatment of the Blessed Virgin Mary,[1] I too wish to begin my reflection on the role of Mary in the mystery of Christ and on her active and exemplary presence in the life of the Church. For they are words which celebrate together the love of the Father, the mission of the Son, the gift of the Spirit, the role of the woman from whom the Redeemer was born, and our own divine filiation, in the mystery of the "fullness of time."[2]

This "fullness" indicates the moment fixed from all eternity when the Father sent his Son "that whoever believes in him should not perish but have eternal life" (Jn 3:16). It denotes the blessed moment when the Word that "was with God . . . became flesh and dwelt among us" (Jn 1:1, 14), and made himself our brother. It marks the moment when the Holy Spirit, who had already infused the fullness of grace into Mary of Nazareth, formed in her virginal womb the human nature of Christ. This "fullness" marks the moment when, with the entrance of the eternal into time, time itself is redeemed, and being filled with the mystery of Christ becomes definitively "salvation time." Finally, this "fullness" designates the hidden beginning of the Church's journey. In the liturgy the Church salutes Mary of Nazareth as the Church's own beginning,[3] for in the event of the Immaculate Conception the Church sees projected, and anticipated in her most noble member, the saving grace of Easter. And above all, in the Incarnation she encounters Christ and Mary indissolubly joined: he who is the Church's Lord and Head and she who, uttering the first *fiat* of the New Covenant, prefigures the Church's condition as spouse and mother.

2. Strengthened by the presence of Christ (cf. Mt 28:20), the Church journeys through time toward the consummation of the ages and goes to meet the Lord who comes. But on this journey—and I wish to make this point straightaway—she proceeds along the path already trodden by the Virgin Mary, who *"advanced in her pilgrimage of faith, and loyally persevered in her union with her Son unto the cross."*[4] I take these very rich and evocative words from the Constitution *Lumen Gentium,* which in its concluding part offers a clear summary of the Church's doctrine on the Mother of Christ, whom she venerates as her beloved Mother and as her model in faith, hope, and charity.

Shortly after the Council, my great predecessor Paul VI decided to speak further of the Blessed Virgin. In the

Encyclical Epistle *Christi Matri* and subsequently in the Apostolic Exhortations *Signum Magnum* and *Marialis Cultus*,[5] he expounded the foundations and criteria of the special veneration which the Mother of Christ receives in the Church, as well as the various forms of Marian devotion—liturgical, popular, and private—which respond to the spirit of faith.

3. The circumstance which now moves me to take up this subject once more *is the prospect of the year 2000,* now drawing near, in which the bimillennial jubilee of the birth of Jesus Christ at the same time directs our gaze toward his Mother. In recent years, various opinions have been voiced suggesting that it would be fitting to precede that anniversary by a similar jubilee in celebration of the birth of Mary.

In fact, even though it is not possible to establish an exact *chronological point* for identifying the date of Mary's birth, the Church has constantly been aware that *Mary appeared* on the horizon of *salvation history before Christ.*[6] It is a fact that when "the fullness of time" was definitively drawing near—the saving advent of Emmanuel—he who was from eternity destined to be his Mother already existed on earth. The fact that she "preceded" the coming of Christ is reflected every year *in the liturgy of Advent.* Therefore, if to that ancient historical expectation of the Savior we compare these years which are bringing us closer to the end of the second millennium after Christ and to the beginning of the third, it becomes fully comprehensible that in this present period we wish to turn in a special way to her, the one who in the "night" of the Advent expectation began to shine like a true "Morning Star" *(Stella Matutina).* For just as this star, together with the "dawn," precedes the rising of the sun, so Mary from the time of her Immaculate Conception preceded the coming of the Savior, the rising of the "Sun of Justice" in the history of the human race.[7]

Her presence in the midst of Israel—a presence so discreet as to pass almost unnoticed by the eyes of her contemporaries—shone very clearly before the Eternal One, who had associated this hidden "Daughter of Zion" (cf. Zeph 3:14; Zeph 2:10) with the plan of salvation embracing the whole history of humanity. With good reason, then, at the end of this millennium, we Christians, who know that the providential plan of the Most Holy Trinity is *the central reality of revelation and of faith*, feel the need to emphasize the unique presence of the Mother of Christ in history, especially during these last years leading up to the year 2000.

4. The Second Vatican Council prepares us for this by presenting in its teaching *the Mother of God in the mystery of Christ and of the Church*. If it is true, as the Council itself proclaims,[8] that "only in the mystery of the incarnate Word does the mystery of man take on light," then this principle must be applied in a very particular way to that exceptional "daughter of the human race," that extraordinary "woman" who became the Mother of Christ. Only *in the mystery of Christ* is *her mystery fully made clear*. Thus has the Church sought to interpret it from the very beginning: the mystery of the Incarnation has enabled her to penetrate and to make ever clearer the mystery of the Mother of the incarnate Word. The Council of Ephesus (431) was of decisive importance in clarifying this, for during that Council, to the great joy of Christians, the truth of the divine motherhood of Mary was solemnly confirmed as a truth of the

Church's faith. Mary *is the Mother of God (= Theotókos)*, since by the power of the Holy Spirit she conceived in her virginal womb and brought into the world Jesus Christ, the Son of God, who is of one being with the Father.[9] "The Son of God . . . born of the Virgin Mary . . . has truly been made one of us," [10] has been made man. Thus, through the mystery of Christ, on the horizon of the Church's faith there shines in its fullness the mystery of his Mother. In turn, the dogma of the divine motherhood of Mary was for the Council of Ephesus and is for the Church like a seal upon the dogma of the Incarnation, in which the Word truly assumes human nature into the unity of his person, without canceling out that nature.

5. The Second Vatican Council, by presenting Mary in the mystery of Christ, also finds the path to a deeper understanding of the mystery of the Church. Mary, as the Mother of Christ, *is in a particular way united with the Church*, "which the Lord established as his own body." [11] It is significant that the conciliar text places this truth about the Church as the Body of Christ (according to the teaching of the Pauline Letters) in close proximity to the truth that the Son of God "through the power of the Holy Spirit was born of the Virgin Mary." The reality of the Incarnation finds a sort of extension *in the mystery of the Church—the Body of Christ*. And one cannot think of the reality of the Incarnation without referring to Mary, the Mother of the incarnate Word.

In these reflections, however, I wish to consider primarily that "pilgrimage of faith" in which "the Blessed Virgin advanced," faithfully preserving her union with Christ.[12] In this way the *"twofold bond"* which unites the Mother of God *with Christ and with the Church* takes on historical significance. Nor is it just a question of the Virgin Mother's life story, of her personal journey of faith and "the better part" which is hers in the mystery of salvation; it is also a question of the history of the whole People of God, *of all those who take part* in the same "*pilgrimage of faith.*"

The Council expresses this when it states in another passage that Mary "has gone before," becoming "a model of the Church in the matter of faith, charity, and perfect union with Christ."[13] This "*going before*" *as a figure or model* is in reference to the intimate mystery of the Church, as she actuates and accomplishes her own saving mission by uniting in herself—as Mary did—the qualities *of mother and virgin.* She is a virgin who "keeps whole and pure the fidelity she has pledged to her Spouse" and "becomes herself a mother," for "she brings forth to a new and immortal life children who are conceived of the Holy Spirit and born of God."[14]

6. All this is accomplished in a great historical process, comparable "to a journey." *The pilgrimage of faith indicates the interior history*, that is, the story of souls. But it is also the story of all human beings, subject here on earth to transitoriness, and part of the historical dimension. In the following reflections we wish to concentrate first of all on the present, which in itself is not yet history, but which nevertheless is constantly forming it, also in the sense of the history of salvation. Here there opens up a broad prospect, within which the *Blessed Virgin Mary continues to "go before" the People of God.* Her exceptional pilgrimage of faith represents a constant point of reference for the Church, for individuals and for communities,

for peoples and nations, and, in a sense, for all humanity. It is indeed difficult to encompass and measure its range.

The Council emphasizes that *the Mother of God is already the eschatological fulfillment of the Church*: "In the most holy Virgin the Church has already reached that perfection whereby she exists without spot or wrinkle (cf. Eph 5:27)"; and at the same time the Council says that "the followers of Christ still strive to increase in holiness by conquering sin, and so *they raise their eyes to Mary*, who shines forth to the whole community of the elect as a model of the virtues."[15] The pilgrimage of faith no longer belongs to the Mother of the Son of God: glorified at the side of her Son in heaven, Mary has already crossed the threshold between faith and that vision which is "face to face" (1 Cor 13:12). At the same time, however, in this eschatological fulfillment, Mary does not cease to be the "Star of the Sea" (*Maris Stella*)[16] for all those who are still on the journey of faith. If they lift their eyes to her from their earthly existence, they do so because "the Son whom she brought forth is he whom God placed as the firstborn among many brethren (Rom 8:29),"[17] and also because "in the birth and development" of these brothers and sisters "she cooperates with a maternal love."[18]

PONDER

John Paul II was relatively young when he was elected Pope in 1978. Looming on the horizon was the 2000th birthday of the Redeemer, Jesus Christ—the Way, Truth, and Life not only of the past but of the future. The Pope began immediately to make long-term plans for this grand celebration.

Karol Józef Wojtyła had grown up under totalitarian regimes. His own rise to the cardinalate was in part due to his gentle but firm ability to keep the Catholic faith strong and fervent in the midst of overt oppression. Wojtyła preached that Jesus, the Healer, Teacher, and Savior, gives life its grand and precious meaning. No matter what sins and failures darkened the Church's two thousand year story, Jesus remained its origin and focal point, God-made-man among us to teach us how to live life in the abundance of goodness. The newly elected Pope knew well the dangers of materialism and of a philosophy that valued human life only insofar as it was useful to the productive machine.

Jesus Christ did not stand alone. He selected followers, and he laid down his life for them. At first only a handful listened to him, followed him, loved him—especially his mother. To celebrate Jesus's 2000th birthday meant to listen to, follow, and love Jesus once again with the fervor of that first generation. It also meant to celebrate those who followed him, particularly the chosen woman who agreed to give him flesh and blood, the woman who was with him from the first moments of his life and beyond death—Mary, his constant companion and associate then and now in the entire work of redemption.

1. The Apostle Paul's writings are thought to be the first Scriptures of the New Covenant. How does Paul refer to Mary? How does John Paul II interpret this? (See par. 1)

2. If you had never heard about Mary before reading this document, who would you say she is? What is her role? (par. 1ff.)

3. Mary's womb fills with the little life of God's Son. In Mary and through her, time reaches its fullness. The Savior—the reason for time, for eternity, and for our human existence—is given a home among us. How can Christians share Mary's birthing role? (par. 2)

4. The Church venerates the Mother of Christ "as her beloved Mother and as her model in faith, hope, and charity." How does your parish and your community express love for Mary? And how do *you* express your love for Mary? (par. 2)

Pray

Mary, all generations admire you, wonder about you, and ask questions about you. Did you then and do you now think of such things as a *precise role, a role of the woman*, or *of being saluted?* While you walked from Nazareth on so many journeys, did you sense that thousands would try to walk in your footsteps of faith, longing to have your ability to believe, to hope, and to love? Your love was not just for the Baby in your womb and in your arms—but for *everyone*, including me. Did you ever realize you were a dawn announcing the Sun of Justice?

I want to stand quietly in a corner of your dwelling and observe just one day, any day, to see what you do and how you do it. We will never quite understand what it must have been like to observe your pregnancy grow full with mystery. How could such a tiny baby boy be God within you? But then, isn't it true that in our baptismal adoption, we, too, are given an abundance of graced life to grow to fullness? And as you did, aren't we asked to bear him, to bring him and his saving word to a saturated world?

Act

Shun not the divine life offered in the sacraments of the Church. Share these graced gifts lavishly.

PART I

Mary in the Mystery of Christ

Full of grace

7. "Blessed be the God and Father of our Lord Jesus Christ, who has blessed us in Christ with every spiritual blessing in the heavenly places" (Eph 1:3). These words of the *Letter to the Ephesians* reveal the eternal design of God the Father, his plan of man's salvation in Christ. It is a universal plan, which concerns all men and women created in the image and likeness of God (cf. Gen 1:26). Just as all are included in the creative work of God "in the beginning," so all are eternally included in the divine plan of salvation, which is to be completely revealed, in the "fullness of time," with the final coming of Christ. In fact, the God who is the "Father of our Lord Jesus Christ"—these are the next words of the same *Letter*—*"chose us in him before the foundation of the world,* that we should be holy and blameless before him. He destined us in love to be his sons through Jesus Christ, according to the purpose of his will, to the praise of his glorious grace, which he freely bestowed on us in *the Beloved.* In

him we have redemption through his blood, the forgiveness of our trespasses, according to the riches of his grace" (Eph 1:4–7).

The divine plan of salvation—which was fully revealed to us with the coming of Christ—is eternal. And according to the teaching contained in the *Letter* just quoted and in other Pauline Letters (cf. Col 1:12–14; Rom 3:24; Gal 3:13; 2 Cor 5:18–29), it is also *eternally linked to Christ.* It includes everyone, but it reserves a special place for the *"woman"* who is the Mother of him to whom the Father has entrusted the work of salvation.[19] As the Second Vatican Council says, "she is already prophetically foreshadowed in that promise made to our first parents after their fall into sin"—according to the *Book of Genesis* (cf. 3:15). "Likewise she is the Virgin who is to conceive and bear a son, whose name will be called Emmanuel" —according to the words of Isaiah (cf. 7:14).[20] In this way the Old Testament prepares that "fullness of time" when God "sent forth his Son, born of woman . . . so that we might receive adoption as sons." The coming into the world of the Son of God is an event recorded in the first chapters of the Gospels according to Luke and Matthew.

8. *Mary* is definitively *introduced into the mystery of Christ through* this event: *the annunciation* by the angel. This takes place at Nazareth, within the concrete circumstances of the history of Israel, the people that first received God's promises. The divine messenger says to the Virgin: "Hail, full of grace, the Lord is with you" (Lk 1:28). Mary "was greatly troubled at the saying, and considered in her mind what sort of greeting this might be" (Lk 1:29): what could those extraordinary

words mean, and in particular the expression "full of grace" (*kécharitôménê*)?[21]

If we wish to meditate together with Mary on these words, and especially on the expression "full of grace," we can find a significant echo in the very passage from the *Letter to the Ephesians* quoted above. And if after the announcement of the heavenly messenger the Virgin of Nazareth is also called "blessed among women" (cf. Lk 1:42), it is because of that blessing with which "God the Father" has filled us "in the heavenly places, in Christ." It is a *spiritual blessing* which is meant for all people and which bears in itself fullness and universality ("every blessing"). It flows from that love which, in the Holy Spirit, unites the consubstantial Son to the Father. At the same time, it is a blessing poured out through Jesus Christ upon human history until the end: upon all people. This blessing, however, refers *to Mary in a special and exceptional degree:* for she was greeted by Elizabeth as "blessed among women."

The double greeting is due to the fact that in the soul of this "daughter of Zion" there is manifested, in a sense, all the "glory of grace," that grace which "the Father . . . has given us in his beloved Son." For the messenger greets Mary as "full of grace"; he calls her thus as if it were her real name. He does not call her by her proper earthly name: Miryam (= Mary), but *by this new name: "full of grace."* What does this name mean? Why does the archangel address the Virgin of Nazareth in this way?

In the language of the Bible "grace" means a special gift, which according to the New Testament has its source precisely in the Trinitarian life of God himself, God who is love (cf. 1 Jn 4:8). The fruit of this love is "*the election*" of which the *Letter to the Ephesians* speaks. On the part of God, this election is the eternal desire to save man through a sharing in his own life (cf. 2 Pt 1:4) in Christ: it is salvation through a sharing in supernatural life. The effect of this eternal gift, of this grace of man's election by God, is like a *seed of holiness,* or a spring which rises in the soul as a gift from God himself, who through grace gives life and holiness to those who are chosen. In this way there is fulfilled, that is to say there comes about, that "blessing" of man "with every spiritual blessing," that "being his adopted sons and daughters . . . in Christ," in him who is eternally the "beloved Son" of the Father.

When we read that the messenger addresses Mary as "full of grace," the Gospel context, which mingles revelations and ancient promises, enables us to understand that among all the "spiritual blessings in Christ" this is a special "blessing." In the mystery of Christ she is *present* even "before the creation of the world," as the one whom the Father "has chosen" *as Mother* of his Son in the Incarnation. And, what is more, together with the Father, the Son has chosen her, entrusting her eternally to the Spirit of holiness. In an entirely special and exceptional way Mary is united to Christ, and similarly she *is eternally loved in this "beloved Son,"* this Son who is of one being with the Father, in whom is concentrated all the "glory of grace." At the same time, she is and remains perfectly open to this "gift from above" (cf. Jas 1:17). As the Council teaches, Mary "stands out among the poor and humble of the Lord, who confidently await and receive salvation from him."[22]

9. If the greeting and the name "full of grace" say all this, in the context of the angel's announcement they refer first of all *to the election of Mary as Mother of the Son of God.* But at the same time the "fullness of grace" indicates all the supernatural munificence from which Mary benefits by being chosen and destined to be the Mother of Christ. If this election is fundamental for the accomplishment of God's salvific designs for humanity, and if the eternal choice in Christ and the vocation to the dignity of adopted children is the destiny of everyone, then the election of Mary is wholly exceptional and unique. Hence also the singularity and uniqueness of her place in the mystery of Christ.

The divine messenger says to her: "Do not be afraid, Mary, for you have found favor with God. And behold, you will conceive in your womb and bear a son, and you shall call his name Jesus. He will be great, and will be called the Son of the Most High" (Lk 1:30–32). And when the Virgin, disturbed by that extraordinary greeting, asks: "How shall this be, since I have no husband?" she receives from the angel the confirmation and explanation of the preceding words. Gabriel says to her: *"The Holy Spirit will come upon you,* and the power of the Most High will overshadow you; therefore the child to be born will be called holy, the Son of God" (Lk 1:35).

The annunciation, therefore, is the revelation of the mystery of the Incarnation at the very beginning of its fulfillment on earth. God's salvific giving of himself and his life, in some way to all creation but directly to man, reaches *one of its high points in the mystery of the Incarnation.* This is indeed a high point among all the gifts of grace conferred in the history of man and of the universe: Mary is "full of grace," because it is precisely in her that the Incarnation of the Word, the hypostatic union of the Son of God with human nature, is accomplished and fulfilled. As the Council says, Mary is "the Mother of the Son of God. As a result she is also the favorite daughter of the Father and the temple of the Holy Spirit. Because of this gift of sublime grace, she far surpasses all other creatures, both in heaven and on earth."[23]

10. The *Letter to the Ephesians,* speaking of the "glory of grace" that "God, the Father . . . has bestowed on us in his beloved Son," adds: "In him we have redemption through his blood" (Eph 1:7). According to the belief formulated in solemn documents of the Church, this "glory of grace" is manifested in the Mother of God through the fact that she has been "redeemed in a more sublime manner."[24] By virtue of the richness of the grace of the beloved Son, by reason of the redemptive merits of him who willed to become her Son, Mary was *preserved from the inheritance of original sin.*[25] In this way, from the first moment of her conception—which is to say of her existence—she belonged to Christ, sharing in the salvific and sanctifying grace and in that love which has its beginning in the "Beloved," the Son of the Eternal Father, who through the Incarnation became her own Son. Consequently, through the power of the Holy Spirit, in the order of grace, which is a participation in the divine nature, *Mary receives life from him to whom she herself,* in the order of earthly generation, *gave life* as a mother. The liturgy does not hesitate to call her "mother of her Creator"[26] and to hail her with the words which Dante Alighieri places on the lips of St. Bernard:

"daughter of your Son."[27] And since Mary receives this "new life" with a fullness corresponding to the Son's love for the Mother, and thus corresponding to the dignity of the divine motherhood, the angel at the annunciation calls her "full of grace."

11. In the salvific design of the Most Holy Trinity, the mystery of the Incarnation constitutes the superabundant *fulfillment of the promise* made by God to man *after original sin,* after that first sin whose effects oppress the whole earthly history of man (cf. Gen 3:15). And so, there comes into the world a Son, "the seed of the woman" who will crush the evil of sin in its very origins: "he will crush the head of the serpent." As we see from the words of the Proto-gospel, the victory of the woman's Son will not take place without a hard struggle, a struggle that is to extend through the whole of human history. The "enmity," foretold at the beginning, is confirmed in the Apocalypse (the book of the final events of the Church and the world), in which there recurs the sign of the "woman," this time "clothed with the sun" (Rev 12:1).

Mary, Mother of the incarnate Word, is placed *at the very center of that enmity,* that struggle which accompanies the history of humanity on earth and the history of salvation itself. In this central place, she who belongs to the "weak and poor of the Lord" bears in herself, like no other member of the human race, that "glory of grace" which the Father "has bestowed on us in his beloved Son," and this *grace determines the extraordinary greatness and beauty* of her whole being. Mary thus remains before God, and also before the whole of humanity, as the unchangeable and inviolable sign of God's election, spoken of in Paul's letter: "in Christ ... he chose us ... before the foundation of the world ... he destined us ... to be his sons" (Eph 1:4, 5). This election is more powerful than any experience of evil and sin, than all that "enmity" which marks the history of man. In this history Mary remains a sign of sure hope.

Blessed is she who believed

12. Immediately after the narration of the annunciation, the Evangelist Luke guides us in the footsteps of the Virgin of Nazareth toward "a city of Judah" (Lk 1:39). According to scholars this city would be the modern Ain Karim, situated in the mountains, not far from Jerusalem. Mary arrived there "in haste," *to visit Elizabeth* her kinswoman. The reason for her visit is also to be found in the fact that at the annunciation Gabriel had made special mention of Elizabeth, who in her old age had conceived a son by her husband Zechariah, through the power of God: "Your kinswoman Elizabeth in her old age has also conceived a son; and this is the sixth month with her who was called barren. *For with God nothing will be impossible*" (Lk 1:36–37). The divine messenger had spoken of what had been accomplished in Elizabeth in order to answer Mary's question. "How shall this be, since I have no husband?" (Lk 1:34). It is to come to pass precisely through the "power of the Most High," just as it happened in the case of Elizabeth, and even more so.

Moved by charity, therefore, Mary goes to the house of her kinswoman. When Mary enters, Elizabeth replies to her greeting and feels the child leap in her womb, and being "filled with the Holy Spirit" she *greets Mary* with a loud cry: "Blessed are you among women, and blessed is the fruit of your womb!" (cf. Lk 1:40–42). Elizabeth's exclamation or acclamation was subsequently to become part of the *Hail Mary,* as a continuation of the angel's greeting, thus becoming one of the Church's most frequently used prayers. But still more significant are the words of Elizabeth in the question which follows: "And why is this granted me, that the mother of my Lord should come to me?" (Lk 1:43). Elizabeth bears witness to Mary: she recognizes and proclaims that before her stands the Mother of the Lord, the Mother of the messiah. The son whom Elizabeth is carrying in her womb also shares in this witness: "The babe in my womb leaped for joy" (Lk 1:44). This child is the future John the Baptist, who at the Jordan will point out Jesus as the messiah.

While every word of Elizabeth's greeting is filled with meaning, her final words would seem to have *fundamental importance:* "And blessed is she who believed that there would be a fulfillment of what was spoken to her from the Lord" (Lk 1:45).[28] These words can be linked with the title "full of grace" of the angel's greeting. Both of these texts reveal an essential Mariological content, namely the truth about Mary, who has become really present in the mystery of Christ precisely because she "has believed." The *fullness of grace* announced by the angel means the gift of God himself. *Mary's faith,* proclaimed by Elizabeth at the visitation, indicates *how* the Virgin of Nazareth *responded to this gift.*

13. As the Council teaches, "'The obedience of faith' (Rom 16:26; cf. Rom 1:5; 2 Cor 10:5–6) must be given to God who

reveals, an obedience by which man entrusts his whole self freely to God."[29] This description of faith found perfect realization in Mary. The "decisive" moment was the annunciation, and the very words of Elizabeth: "And blessed is she who believed" refer primarily to that very moment.[30]

Indeed, at the annunciation Mary entrusted herself to God completely, with the "full submission of intellect and will," manifesting "the obedience of faith" to him who spoke to her through his messenger.[31] She responded, therefore, *with all her human and feminine "I,"* and this response of faith included both perfect cooperation with "the grace of God that precedes and assists" and perfect openness to the action of the Holy Spirit, who "constantly brings faith to completion by his gifts."[32]

The word of the living God, announced to Mary by the angel, referred to her: "And behold, you will conceive in your womb and bear a son" (Lk 1:31). By accepting this announcement, Mary was to become the "Mother of the Lord," and the divine mystery of the Incarnation was to be accomplished in her: "The Father of mercies willed that the consent of the predestined Mother should precede the Incarnation."[33] And Mary gives this consent, after she has heard everything the messenger has to say. She says: "Behold, I am the handmaid of the Lord; let it be to me according to your word" (Lk 1:38). This *fiat* of Mary—"let it be to me"—was decisive, on the human level, for the accomplishment of the divine mystery. There is a complete harmony with the words of the Son, who, according to the *Letter to the Hebrews,* says to the Father as he comes into the world: "Sacrifices and offering you have not desired, but *a body you have prepared for me. . . .* Lo, I have come to do your will, O God" (Heb 10:5–7). The mystery of the Incarnation was accomplished when Mary uttered her *fiat*: "Let it be to me according to your word," which made possible, as far as it depended upon her in the divine plan, the granting of her Son's desire.

Mary uttered this *fiat in faith.* In faith she entrusted herself to God without reserve and "devoted herself totally as the handmaid of the Lord to the person and work of her Son."[34] And as the Fathers of the Church teach—she conceived this Son in her mind before she conceived him in her womb: precisely in faith![35] Rightly, therefore, does Elizabeth praise Mary: "And blessed is she who believed *that there would be a fulfillment* of what was spoken to her from the Lord." These words have already been fulfilled: Mary of Nazareth presents herself at the threshold of Elizabeth and Zechariah's house as the Mother of the Son of God. This is Elizabeth's joyful discovery: "The mother of my Lord comes to me"!

14. Mary's faith can also be *compared to that of Abraham,* whom St. Paul calls "our father in faith" (cf. Rom 4:12). In the salvific economy of God's revelation, Abraham's faith constitutes the beginning of the Old Covenant; Mary's faith at the annunciation inaugurates the New Covenant. Just as Abraham *"in hope believed against hope,* that he should become the father of many nations" (cf. Rom 4:18), so Mary, at the annunciation, having professed her virginity ("How shall this be, since I have no husband?") *believed* that through the power of the Most High, by the power of the Holy Spirit, she would become the Mother of God's Son in accordance with the

angel's revelation: "The child to be born will be called holy, the Son of God" (Lk 1:35).

However, Elizabeth's words "And blessed is she who believed" do not apply only to that particular moment of the annunciation. Certainly the annunciation is the culminating moment of Mary's faith in her awaiting of Christ, but it is also the point of departure from which her whole "journey toward God" begins, her whole pilgrimage of faith. And on this road, in an eminent and truly heroic manner—indeed with an ever greater heroism of faith—the "obedience" which she professes to the word of divine revelation will be fulfilled. Mary's "obedience of faith" during the whole of her pilgrimage will show surprising similarities to the faith of Abraham. Just like the patriarch of the People of God, so too Mary, during the pilgrimage of her filial and maternal *fiat*, "in hope believed against hope." Especially during certain stages of this journey the blessing granted to her "who believed" will be revealed with particular vividness. To believe means "to abandon oneself" to the truth of the word of the living God, knowing and humbly recognizing "how unsearchable are his judgments and how *inscrutable his ways*" (Rom 11:33). Mary, who by the eternal will of the Most High stands, one may say, at the very center of those "inscrutable ways" and "unsearchable judgments" of God, conforms herself to them in the dim light of faith, accepting fully and with a ready heart everything that is decreed in the divine plan.

15. When at the annunciation Mary hears of the Son whose Mother she is to become and to whom "she will give the name Jesus" (= Savior), she also learns that "the Lord God

will give to him the throne of his father David," and that "he will reign over the house of Jacob forever and of his kingdom there will be no end" (Lk 1:32–33). The hope of the whole of Israel was directed toward this. The promised messiah is to be "great," and the heavenly messenger also announces that *"he will be great"*—great both by bearing the name of *Son of the Most High* and by the fact that he is to assume the *inheritance of David.* He is therefore to be a king; he is to reign "over the house of Jacob." Mary had grown up in the midst of these expectations of her people: could she guess, at the moment of the annunciation, the vital significance of the angel's words? And how is one to understand that "kingdom" which "will have no end"?

Although through faith she may have perceived in that instant she was the mother of the "messiah King," nevertheless she replied: *"Behold, I am the handmaid of the Lord;* let it be to me according to your word" (Lk 1:38). From the first moment Mary professed above all the "obedience of faith," abandoning herself to the meaning which was given to the words of the annunciation by him from whom they proceeded: God himself.

16. Later, a little further along this way of the "obedience of faith," Mary *hears other words*: those uttered by *Simeon* in the Temple of Jerusalem. It was now forty days after the birth of Jesus when, in accordance with the precepts of the Law of Moses, Mary and Joseph "brought him up to Jerusalem to present him to the Lord" (Lk 2:22). The birth had taken place in conditions of extreme poverty. We know from Luke that when, on the occasion of the census ordered by the Roman

authorities, Mary went with Joseph to Bethlehem, having found "no place in the inn," *she gave birth to her Son in a stable* and "laid him in a manger" (cf. Lk 2:7).

A just and God-fearing man called Simeon appears at this beginning of Mary's "journey" of faith. His words, suggested by the Holy Spirit (cf. Lk 2:25–27), confirm the truth of the annunciation. For we read that he took up in his arms the child to whom—in accordance with the angel's command—the name Jesus was given (cf. Lk 2:21). Simeon's words match the meaning of this name, which is Savior: "God is salvation." Turning to the Lord, he says: "For my eyes have seen your *salvation* which you have prepared *in the presence of all peoples*, a light for revelation to the Gentiles, and for glory to your people Israel" (Lk 2:30–32). At the same time, however, Simeon addresses Mary with the following words: "Behold, this child is set for the fall and rising of many in Israel, and for a *sign that is spoken against*, that thoughts out of many hearts may be revealed"; and he adds with direct reference to her: "and a sword will pierce through your own soul also" (cf. Lk 2:34–35). Simeon's words cast new light on the announcement which Mary had heard from the angel: Jesus is the Savior, he is "a *light* for revelation" to mankind. Is not this what was manifested in a way on Christmas night, when the *shepherds* came to the stable (cf. Lk 2:8–20)? Is not this what was to be manifested even more clearly in the coming of the *Magi from the East* (cf. Mt 2:1–12)? But at the same time, at the very beginning of his life, the Son of Mary, and his Mother with him, will experience in themselves the truth of those other words of Simeon: "a sign that is spoken against" (Lk

2:34). Simeon's words seem like a *second annunciation to Mary*, for they tell her of the actual historical situation in which the Son is to accomplish his mission, namely, in misunderstanding and sorrow. While this announcement on the one hand confirms her faith in the accomplishment of the divine promises of salvation, on the other hand it also reveals to her that she will have to live her obedience of faith in suffering, at the side of the suffering Savior, and that her motherhood will be mysterious and sorrowful. Thus, after the visit of the Magi who came from the East, after their homage ("they fell down and worshipped him") and after they had offered gifts (cf. Mt 2:11), Mary together with the child *has to flee into Egypt* in the protective care of Joseph, for "Herod is about to search for the child, to destroy him" (cf. Mt 2:13). And until the death of Herod they will have to remain in Egypt (cf. Mt 2:15).

17. When the Holy Family returns to Nazareth after Herod's death, there begins the long *period of the hidden life.* She "who believed that there would be a fulfillment of what was spoken to her from the Lord" (Lk 1:45) lives the reality of these words day by day. And daily at her side is the Son to whom "*she gave the name Jesus*"; therefore in contact with him she certainly uses this name, a fact which would have surprised no one, since the name had long been in use in Israel. Nevertheless, Mary knows that he who bears the name *Jesus has been called by the angel "the Son of the Most High*" (cf. Lk 1:32). Mary knows she has conceived and given birth to him "without having a husband," by the power of the Holy Spirit, by the power of the Most High who overshadowed her (cf. Lk 1:35), just as at the time of Moses and the patriarchs the cloud

covered the presence of God (cf. Ex 24:16; 40:34–35; 1 Kgs 8:10–12). Therefore Mary knows that the Son to whom she gave birth in a virginal manner is precisely that "Holy One," the Son of God, of whom the angel spoke to her.

During the years of Jesus' hidden life in the house at Nazareth, *Mary's life* too is *"hidden with Christ in God"* (cf. Col 3:3) *through faith.* For faith is contact with the mystery of God. Every day Mary is in constant contact with the ineffable mystery of God made man, a mystery that surpasses everything revealed in the Old Covenant. From the moment of the annunciation, the mind of the Virgin Mother has been initiated into the radical "newness" of God's self-revelation and has been made aware of the mystery. She is the first of those "little ones" of whom Jesus will say one day: "Father . . . you have hidden these things from the wise and understanding and revealed them to babes" (Mt 11:25). For "no one knows the Son except the Father" (Mt 11:27). If this is the case, how can Mary "know the Son"? Of course she does not know him as the Father does, and yet she is *the first of those to whom the Father "has chosen to reveal him"* (cf. Mt 11:26–27; 1 Cor 2:11). If though, from the moment of the annunciation, the Son— whom only the Father knows completely, as the one who begets him in the eternal "today" (cf. Ps 2:7) was revealed to Mary, she, his Mother, is in contact with the truth about her Son only in faith and through faith! She is therefore blessed, because "she has believed," and continues to *believe day after day* amidst all the trials and the adversities of Jesus' infancy and then during the years of the hidden life at Nazareth, where he "was obedient to them" (Lk 2:51). He was obedient both to

Mary and also to Joseph, since Joseph took the place of his father in people's eyes; for this reason, the Son of Mary was regarded by the people as "the carpenter's son" (Mt 13:55).

The Mother of *that Son*, therefore, mindful of what has been told her at the annunciation and in subsequent events, bears within herself the radical "newness" of faith: *the beginning of the New Covenant*. This is the beginning of the Gospel, the joyful Good News. However, it is not difficult to see in that beginning *a particular heaviness of heart*, linked with a sort of "night of faith"—to use the words of St. John of the Cross —a kind of "veil" through which one has to draw near to the Invisible One and to live in intimacy with the mystery.[36] And this is the way that Mary, for many years, *lived in intimacy with the mystery of her Son*, and went forward in her "pilgrimage of faith," while Jesus "increased in wisdom . . . and in favor with God and man" (Lk 2:52). God's predilection for him was manifested ever more clearly to people's eyes. The first human creature thus permitted to discover Christ was Mary, who lived with Joseph in the same house at Nazareth.

However, when he had been found in the Temple, and his Mother asked him, "Son, why have you treated us so?" *the twelve-year-old Jesus* answered: "Did you not know that I must be in my Father's house?" And the evangelist adds: "*And they* [Joseph and Mary] *did not understand* the saying which he spoke to them" (Lk 2:48–50). Jesus was aware that "no one knows the Son except the Father" (cf. Mt 11:27); thus even his Mother, to whom had been revealed most completely the mystery of his divine sonship, lived in intimacy with this mystery only through faith! Living side by side with her Son under the same roof, and faithfully persevering "in her union with her Son," she "*advanced in her pilgrimage of faith*," as the Council emphasizes.[37] And so it was during Christ's public life too (cf. Mk 3:21–35) that day by day there was fulfilled in her the blessing uttered by Elizabeth at the visitation: "Blessed is she who believed."

18. This blessing reaches its full meaning *when Mary stands beneath the cross* of her Son (cf. Jn 19:25). The Council says that this happened "not without a divine plan": by "suffering deeply with her only-begotten Son and joining herself with her maternal spirit to his sacrifice, lovingly consenting to the immolation of the victim to whom she had given birth"; in this way Mary "faithfully preserved her union with her Son even to the cross."[38] It is a union through faith—the same faith with which she had received the angel's revelation at the annunciation. At that moment she had also heard the words: "He will be great . . . and *the Lord God* will give to him the throne of his father David, and he will reign over the house of Jacob forever; and of his kingdom there will be no end" (Lk 1:32–33).

And now, standing at the foot of the cross, Mary is the witness, humanly speaking, of the complete *negation of these words*. On that wood of the cross her Son hangs in agony as one condemned. "He was despised and rejected by men; a man of sorrows . . . he was despised, and we esteemed him not": as one destroyed (cf. Is 53:3–5). How great, how heroic then is the *obedience of faith* shown by Mary in the face of God's "unsearchable judgments"! How completely she "abandons herself to God" without reserve, offering the full assent of the intellect and the will"[39] to him whose "ways are inscrutable" (cf. Rom 11:33)! And how powerful too is the action of grace in her soul, how all-pervading is the influence of the Holy Spirit and of his light and power!

Through this faith Mary is perfectly united with Christ in his self-emptying. For "Christ Jesus, who, though he was in the form of God, did not count equality with God a thing to be grasped, but emptied himself, taking the form of a servant, being born in the likeness of men": precisely on Golgotha "humbled himself and became obedient unto death, even death on a cross" (cf. Phil 2:5–8). At the foot of the cross Mary shares through faith in the shocking mystery of this self-emptying. This is perhaps the deepest *"kenosis" of faith* in human history. Through faith the Mother shares in the death of her Son, in his redeeming death; but in contrast with the faith of the disciples who fled, hers was far more enlightened. On Golgotha, Jesus through the cross definitively confirmed that he was the "sign of contradiction" foretold by Simeon. At the same time, there were also fulfilled on Golgotha the words which Simeon had addressed to Mary: "and a sword will pierce through your own soul also."[40]

19. Yes, truly "blessed is she who believed"! These words, spoken by Elizabeth after the annunciation, here at the foot of the cross seem to re-echo with supreme eloquence, and the power contained within them becomes something penetrating. From the cross, that is to say from the very heart of the mystery of redemption, there radiates and spreads out the prospect of that blessing of faith. It goes right back to "the beginning," and as a sharing in the sacrifice of Christ—the

new Adam—it becomes in a certain sense *the counterpoise to the disobedience and disbelief* embodied in the sin of our first parents. Thus teach the Fathers of the Church and especially St. Irenaeus, quoted by the Constitution *Lumen Gentium:* "The knot of Eve's disobedience was untied by Mary's obedience; what the virgin Eve bound through her unbelief, the Virgin Mary *loosened by her faith*."[41] In the light of this comparison with Eve, the Fathers of the Church—as the Council also says—call Mary the "mother of the living" and often speak of "death through Eve, life through Mary."[42]

In the expression "Blessed is she who believed," we can therefore rightly find *a kind of "key"* which unlocks for us the innermost reality of Mary, whom the angel hailed as "full of grace." If as "full of grace" she has been eternally present in the mystery of Christ, through faith she became a sharer in that mystery in every extension of her earthly journey. She "advanced in her pilgrimage of faith" and at the same time, in a discreet yet direct and effective way, she made present to humanity *the mystery of Christ*. And she still continues to do so. Through the mystery of Christ, she too is present within mankind. Thus through the mystery of the Son the mystery of the Mother is also made clear.

Behold your mother

20. The Gospel of Luke records the moment when "a woman in the crowd raised her voice" and said to Jesus: *"Blessed is the womb that bore you, and the breasts that you sucked!"* (Lk 11:27). These words were an expression of praise of Mary as

Jesus' mother according to the flesh. Probably the Mother of Jesus was not personally known to this woman; in fact, when Jesus began his messianic activity Mary did not accompany him but continued to remain at Nazareth. One could say that the words of that unknown woman in a way brought Mary out of her hiddenness.

Through these words, there flashed out in the midst of the crowd, at least for an instant, the gospel of Jesus' infancy. This is the gospel in which Mary is present as the mother who conceives Jesus in her womb, gives him birth, and nurses him: the nursing mother referred to by the woman in the crowd. *Thanks to this motherhood, Jesus,* the Son of the Most High (cf. Lk 1:32), is a true *son of man.* He is "flesh," like every other man: he is "the Word (who) became flesh" (cf. Jn 1:14). He is of the flesh and blood of Mary![43]

But to the blessing uttered by that woman upon her, who was his mother according to the flesh, Jesus replies in a significant way: "Blessed rather are *those who hear the Word of God and keep it*" (Lk 11:28). He wishes to divert attention from motherhood understood only as a fleshly bond, in order to direct it toward those mysterious bonds of the spirit which develop from hearing and keeping God's word.

This same shift into the sphere of spiritual values is seen even more clearly in another response of Jesus reported by all the synoptics. When Jesus is told that "his mother and brothers are standing outside and wish to see him," he replies: *"My mother and my brothers are those who hear the word of God and do it"* (cf. Lk 8:20–21). This he said "looking around on those who sat about him," as we read in Mark (3:34) or, according to Matthew (12:49), "stretching out his hand toward his disciples."

These statements seem to *fit in with the reply which the twelve-year-old Jesus* gave to Mary and Joseph when he was found after three days in the Temple at Jerusalem.

Now, when Jesus left Nazareth and began his public life throughout Palestine, *he was completely and exclusively "concerned with his Father's business"* (cf. Lk 2:49). He announced the kingdom: the "kingdom of God" and "his Father's business," which add a new dimension and meaning to everything human, and therefore to every human bond, insofar as these things relate to the goals and tasks assigned to every human being. Within this new dimension, also a bond such as that of "brotherhood" means something different from "brotherhood according to the flesh" deriving from a common origin from the same set of parents. "*Motherhood*," too, *in the dimension of the kingdom of God and in the radius of the fatherhood of God himself, takes on another meaning.* In the words reported by Luke, Jesus teaches precisely this new meaning of motherhood.

Is Jesus thereby distancing himself from his mother according to the flesh? Does he perhaps wish to leave her in the hidden obscurity which she herself has chosen? If this seems to be the case from the tone of those words, one must nevertheless note that the new and different motherhood which Jesus speaks of to his disciples refers precisely to Mary in a very special way. Is not Mary *the first of "those who hear the Word of God and do it"?* And therefore does not the blessing uttered by Jesus in response to the woman in the crowd refer primarily to her? Without any doubt, Mary is worthy of blessing by the very fact that she became the mother of Jesus according to the flesh ("Blessed is the womb that bore you, and the breasts that you sucked"), but also and especially because already at the annunciation she accepted the Word of God, because she believed it, *because she was obedient to God,* and because she "kept" the word and "pondered it in her heart" (cf. Lk 1:38, 45; 2:19, 51) and by means of her whole life accomplished it. Thus we can say that the blessing proclaimed by Jesus is not in opposition, despite appearances, to the blessing uttered by the unknown woman, but rather coincides with that blessing in the person of this Virgin Mother, who called herself only "the handmaid of the Lord" (Lk 1:38). If it is true that "all generations will call her blessed" (cf. Lk 1:48), then it can be said that the unnamed woman was the first to confirm unwittingly that prophetic phrase of Mary's Magnificat and to begin the Magnificat of the ages.

If *through faith* Mary became the bearer of the Son given to her by the Father through the power of the Holy Spirit, while preserving her virginity intact, in that same faith she *discovered and accepted the other dimension of motherhood* revealed by Jesus during his messianic mission. One can say that this dimension of motherhood belonged to Mary from the beginning, that is to say from the moment of the conception and birth of her Son. From that time she was "the one who believed." But as the messianic mission of her Son grew clearer to her eyes and spirit, she herself as a mother became ever more open *to that new dimension of motherhood* which was to constitute her "part" beside her Son. Had she not said from the very beginning: "Behold, I am the handmaid of the Lord; let it be to me according to your word" (Lk 1:38)? Through faith Mary continued to hear and to ponder that word, in which there became ever clearer, in a way "which surpasses knowledge" (Eph 3:19), the self-revelation of the living God. Thus *in a sense* Mary as Mother became *the first "disciple" of her Son*, the first to whom he seemed to say: "Follow me," even before he addressed this call to the apostles or to anyone else (cf. Jn 1:43).

21. From this point of view, particularly eloquent is the passage in the *Gospel of John* which presents Mary at the wedding feast of Cana. She appears there as the Mother of Jesus at the beginning of his public life: "There was a *marriage at Cana in Galilee*, and the mother of Jesus was there; Jesus also was invited to the marriage, with his disciples" (Jn 2:1–2). From the text it appears that Jesus and his disciples were invited together with Mary, as if by reason of her presence at the celebration; the Son seems to have been invited because of his mother. We are familiar with the sequence of events which resulted from that invitation, that "beginning of the signs" wrought by Jesus—the water changed into wine—which prompts the evangelist to say that Jesus "manifested his glory, and his disciples believed in him" (Jn 2:11).

Mary is present at Cana in Galilee as the *Mother of Jesus*, and in a significant way she *contributes* to that "beginning of the signs" which reveal the messianic power of her Son. We read: "When the wine gave out, the mother of Jesus said to him, 'They have no wine.' And Jesus said to her, 'O woman, what have you to do with me? My hour has not yet come'" (Jn

2:3–4). In John's Gospel that "hour" means the time appointed by the Father when the Son accomplishes his task and is to be glorified (cf. Jn 7:30; 8:20; 12:23, 27; 13:1; 17:1; 19:27). Even though Jesus' reply to his mother sounds like a refusal (especially if we consider the blunt statement "My hour has not yet come" rather than the question), Mary nevertheless turns to the servants and says to them: "Do whatever he tells you" (Jn 2:5). Then Jesus orders the servants to fill the stone jars with water, and the water becomes wine, better than the wine which has previously been served to the wedding guests.

What deep understanding existed between Jesus and his mother? How can we probe the mystery of their intimate spiritual union? But the fact speaks for itself. It is certain that that event already quite clearly outlines *the new dimension,* the new meaning *of Mary's motherhood.* Her motherhood has a significance which is not exclusively contained in the words of Jesus and in the various episodes reported by the synoptics (Lk 11:27–28; Lk 8:19–21; Mt 12:46–50; Mk 3:31–35). In these texts Jesus means above all to contrast the motherhood resulting from the fact of birth with what this "motherhood" (and also "brotherhood") is to be in the dimension of the kingdom of God, in the salvific radius of God's fatherhood. In John's text, on the other hand, the description of the Cana event outlines what is actually manifested as a new kind of motherhood according to the spirit and not just according to the flesh, that is to say *Mary's solicitude for human beings,* her coming to them in the wide variety of their wants and needs. At Cana in Galilee there is shown only one concrete aspect of human need, apparently a small one of little importance

("They have no wine"). But it has a symbolic value: this coming to the aid of human needs means, at the same time, bringing those needs within the radius of Christ's messianic mission and salvific power. Thus there is a mediation: Mary places herself between her Son and mankind in the reality of their wants, needs, and sufferings. *She puts herself "in the middle,"* that is to say *she acts as a mediatrix not as an outsider, but in her position as mother.* She knows that as such she can point out to her Son the needs of mankind, and in fact, she "has the right" to do so. Her mediation is thus in the nature of intercession: Mary "intercedes" for mankind. And that is not all. As a mother she also *wishes the messianic power of her Son to be manifested,* that salvific power of his which is meant to help man in his misfortunes, to free him from the evil which in various forms and degrees weighs heavily upon his life, precisely as the Prophet Isaiah had foretold about the messiah in the famous passage which Jesus quoted before his fellow townsfolk in Nazareth: "To preach good news to the poor ... to proclaim release to the captives and recovering of sight to the blind ..." (cf. Lk 4:18).

Another essential element of Mary's maternal task is found in her words to the servants: "Do whatever he tells you." *The Mother* of Christ presents herself as the *spokeswoman of her Son's will,* pointing out those things which must be done so that the salvific power of the messiah may be manifested. At Cana, thanks to the intercession of Mary and the obedience of the servants, Jesus begins "his hour." At Cana Mary appears as *believing in Jesus.* Her faith evokes his first "sign" and helps to kindle the faith of the disciples.

22. We can therefore say that in this passage of John's Gospel we find as it were a first manifestation of the truth concerning Mary's maternal care. This truth has also found expression *in the teaching of the Second Vatican Council.* It is important to note how the Council illustrates Mary's maternal role as it relates to the mediation of Christ. Thus we read: "Mary's maternal function toward mankind in no way obscures or diminishes the unique mediation of Christ, but rather shows its efficacy," because "there is one mediator between God and men, the man Christ Jesus" (1 Tm 2:5). This maternal role of Mary flows, according to God's good pleasure, "from the superabundance of the merits of Christ; it is founded on his mediation, absolutely depends on it, and draws all its efficacy from it."[44] It is precisely in this sense that the episode at Cana in Galilee offers us *a sort of first announcement of Mary's mediation,* wholly oriented toward Christ and tending to the revelation of his salvific power.

From the *text of John* it is evident that it is a mediation which is maternal. As the Council proclaims, Mary became "a mother to us in the order of grace." This motherhood in the order of grace flows from her divine motherhood. Because she was, by the design of divine Providence, the mother who nourished the divine Redeemer, Mary became "an associate of unique nobility, and the Lord's humble handmaid," who "cooperated by her obedience, faith, hope, and burning charity in the Savior's work of restoring supernatural life to souls."[45] And "this *maternity of Mary in the order of grace . . .* will last without interruption until the eternal fulfillment of all the elect."[46]

23. If John's description of the event at Cana presents Mary's caring motherhood at the beginning of Christ's messianic activity, another passage from the same Gospel confirms this motherhood in the salvific economy of grace at its crowning moment, namely when Christ's sacrifice on the cross, his Paschal Mystery, is accomplished. John's description is concise: "*Standing by the cross of Jesus* were his mother, and his mother's sister, Mary the wife of Clopas, and Mary Magdalene. When Jesus saw his mother, and the disciple whom he loved standing near, he said to his mother: 'Woman, behold your son!' Then he said to the disciple, 'Behold, your mother!' And from that hour the disciple took her to his own home" (Jn 19:25–27).

Undoubtedly, we find here an expression of the Son's particular solicitude for his Mother, whom he is leaving in such great sorrow. And yet the "testament of Christ's cross" says more. Jesus highlights a new relationship between Mother and Son, the whole truth and reality of which he solemnly confirms. One can say that if Mary's motherhood of the human race had already been outlined, now it is clearly stated and established. It *emerges* from the definitive accomplishment *of the Redeemer's Paschal Mystery.* The Mother of Christ, who stands at the very center of this mystery—a mystery which embraces each individual and all humanity—is given as mother to every single individual and all mankind. The man at the foot of the cross is John, "the disciple whom he loved."[47] But it is not he alone. Following tradition, the Council does not hesitate to call Mary *"the Mother of Christ and mother of mankind"*: since she "belongs to the offspring of Adam she is one with all human beings.... Indeed she is 'clearly the mother of the members of Christ ... since she cooperated out of love so that there might be born in the Church the faithful.'"[48]

And so this "new motherhood of Mary," generated by faith, is *the fruit of the "new" love* which came to definitive maturity in her at the foot of the cross, through her sharing in the redemptive love of her Son.

24. Thus we find ourselves at the very center of the fulfillment of the promise contained in the Proto-gospel: the "seed of the woman ... will crush the head of the serpent" (cf. Gen 3:15). By his redemptive death Jesus Christ conquers the evil of sin and death at its very roots. It is significant that, as he speaks to his mother from the cross, he calls her "woman" and says to her: "Woman, behold your son!" Moreover, he had addressed her by the same term at Cana too (cf. Jn 2:4). How can one doubt that especially now, on Golgotha, this expression goes to the very heart of the mystery of Mary, and indicates the unique *place* which she occupies *in the whole economy of salvation*? As the Council teaches, in Mary "the exalted Daughter of Zion, and after a long expectation of the promise, the times were at length fulfilled and the new dispensation established. All this occurred when the Son of God took a human nature from her, that he might in the mysteries of his flesh free man from sin."[49]

The words uttered by Jesus from the cross signify that *the motherhood* of her who bore Christ finds a "new" continuation *in the Church and through the Church*, symbolized and represented by John. In this way, she who as the one "full of grace" was brought into the mystery of Christ in order to be his

Mother and thus *the Holy Mother of God*, through the Church remains in that mystery as "*the woman*" spoken of by the *Book of Genesis* (3:15) at the beginning and by the *Apocalypse* (12:1) at the end of the history of salvation. In accordance with the eternal plan of Providence, Mary's divine motherhood is to be poured out upon the Church, as indicated by statements of Tradition, according to which Mary's "motherhood" of the Church is the reflection and extension of her motherhood of the Son of God.[50]

According to the Council the very moment of the Church's birth and full manifestation to the world enables us to glimpse this continuity of Mary's motherhood: "Since it pleased God not to manifest solemnly the mystery of the salvation of the human race until he poured forth the Spirit promised by Christ, we see the *apostles* before the day of Pentecost 'continuing with one mind *in prayer* with the women and *Mary the mother of Jesus*, and with his brethren' (Acts 1:14). We see Mary prayerfully imploring the gift of the Spirit, who had already overshadowed her in the annunciation."[51]

And so, in the redemptive economy of grace, brought about through the action of the Holy Spirit, there is a unique correspondence between the moment of the Incarnation of the Word and the moment of the birth of the Church. The person who links these two moments is Mary: *Mary at Nazareth* and *Mary in the upper room at Jerusalem*. In both cases her discreet yet essential presence indicates the path of "birth from the Holy Spirit." Thus she who is present in the mystery of Christ as Mother becomes—by the will of the Son and the power of the Holy Spirit—present in the mystery of the Church. In the Church too she continues to be *a maternal presence*, as is shown by the words spoken from the cross: "Woman, behold your son!"; "Behold, your mother."

Ponder

Who really understands grace? Is it a sudden sensing that I could not have succeeded or done something by myself—the awareness of a gift given? Do we ever know *really* what the giver of a gift meant, felt, or invested to give us this treasure—be it tangible or the treasure of self?

John Paul II says:

> If we wish to meditate together with Mary on these words [full of grace] . . . we can find a significant echo in the very passage from the *Letter to the Ephesians* . . . "Blessed be the God and Father of our Lord Jesus Christ, who has blessed us in Christ with every spiritual blessing in the heavenly places . . . that we should be holy and blameless before him. He destined us in love to be his sons through Jesus Christ, according to the purpose of his will, to the praise of his glorious grace, which he freely bestowed on us in *the Beloved*" (cf. Eph 1:4–7) (par. 7).

Do we really believe that we are created by Love for love? Such is our faith, our firm belief. Our very lives are a gift—hard as that is to comprehend some days. John Paul II teaches us that each one of us is elected—Mary not least!

1. When we honor Mary and understand her as someone who "surpasses all other creatures, both in heaven and

on earth," what does that mean in hands-on/hearts-on terms? Would it shock us if someone asked, "So what?" How would we respond (par. 9)? Can we somehow describe that glory of grace that John Paul II speaks about (par. 11)?

2. Mary believed in the marvelous promises of the Annunciation in the long haul, even when suffering touched her life. Can I too believe in God's promises in the midst of pain (par. 14)?

3. As John Paul II writes: "To believe means 'to abandon oneself' to the truth of the word of the living God, knowing and humbly recognizing 'how unsearchable are his judgments and how *inscrutable his ways*' (Rom 11:33)." For Mary, belief and faith are a call from a God of love who gives her a choice to act or not to act. To obey means to listen. She listens, she believes, she acts upon his call (par. 14). In our world, filled with skepticism and distrust, can we live or even imagine living an obedience of faith? How would we do this?

4. [For private reflection] We read, "During the years of Jesus' hidden life in the house at Nazareth, *Mary's life* too is *'hidden with Christ in God'* (cf. Col 3:3) *through faith*. For faith is contact with the mystery of God." When in my life—in those hidden hours unknown to anyone else—have I experienced this mysterious contact, the awareness of the Father's infinite mercy and goodness (par. 17)?

Pray

Mary, what was your Annunciation experience like? How did you feel during that first wondrous overshadowing, that indwelling of the Son of God in your very body? The Fathers of old tell us you conceived your beloved Son first in faith, before conceiving him in your body. So, did love grow gradually? Did you see the Father's loving hand behind every roadside daisy, every puddle's rainbow?

But that dance of love, that quiet overshadowing, held you for a lifetime! Through it all your love remained steadfast: the roads you traveled, the crossbeam's shadow, the loneliness of age, without him to eat at your table and comfort you with his strong arm. Give me, Mary, a share in the bright glow of your faith.

Act

When you have no will to get up, remember love's first glow, rest in it, examine God's personal call to you in your vocation, renew it, and be the first to love again.

Part II

The Mother of God
at the Center of the Pilgrim Church

The Church, the People of God present in all the nations of the earth

25. "The Church 'like a pilgrim in a foreign land, presses forward amid the persecutions of the world and the consolations of God,'[52] announcing the cross and death of the Lord until he comes (cf. 1 Cor 11:26)."[53] "Israel according to the flesh, which wandered as an exile in the desert, was already called the Church of God (cf. Neh 13:1; Num 20:4; Dt 23:1ff.). Likewise the new Israel . . . is also called the Church of Christ (cf. Mt 16:18). For he has bought it for himself with his blood (Acts 20:28), has filled it with his Spirit, and provided it with those means which befit it as a visible and social unity. *God has gathered together as one all those who in faith look upon Jesus* as the author of salvation and the source of unity and peace, and has established them as Church, that for each and all she may be the visible sacrament of this saving unity."[54]

The Second Vatican Council speaks of the pilgrim Church, establishing an analogy with the Israel of the Old Covenant journeying through the desert. The journey also has an *external character*, visible in the time and space in which it historically takes place. For the Church "is destined to extend to all regions of the earth and so to enter into the history of mankind," but at the same time "she transcends all limits of time and of space."[55] And yet the essential *character* of her pilgrimage is *interior*: it is a question of a *pilgrimage through faith*, by "the power of the risen Lord,"[56] a pilgrimage in the Holy Spirit, given to the Church as the invisible Comforter (*parákletos*) (cf. Jn 14:26; 15:26; 16:7): "Moving forward through trial and tribulation, the Church is strengthened by the power of God's grace promised to her by the Lord, so that . . . moved by the Holy Spirit, she may never cease to renew herself, until through the cross she arrives at the light which knows no setting."[57]

It is precisely *in this ecclesial journey or pilgrimage* through space and time, and even more through the history of souls, that *Mary is present*, as the one who is "blessed because she believed," as the one who advanced on the pilgrimage of faith, sharing unlike any other creature in the mystery of Christ. The Council further says that "Mary figured profoundly in the history of salvation and in a certain way unites and mirrors within herself the central truths of the faith."[58] Among all believers she is *like a "mirror"* in which are reflected in the most profound and limpid way "the mighty works of God" (Acts 2:11).

26. Built by Christ upon the apostles, the Church became fully aware of these mighty works of God *on the day of Pentecost*,

when those gathered together in the upper room "were all filled with the Holy Spirit and began to speak in other tongues, as the Spirit gave them utterance" (Acts 2:4). From that moment there also *begins* that journey of faith, *the Church's pilgrimage* through the history of individuals and peoples. We know that at the beginning of this journey Mary is present. We see her in the midst of the apostles in the upper room, "prayerfully imploring the gift of the Spirit."[59]

In a sense her journey of faith is longer. The Holy Spirit had already come down upon her, and she became his faithful spouse *at the annunciation*, welcoming the Word of the true God, offering "the full submission of intellect and will . . . and freely assenting to the truth revealed by him," indeed abandoning herself totally to God through "the obedience of faith,"[60] whereby she replied to the angel: "Behold, I am the handmaid of the Lord; let it be to me according to your word." The journey of faith made by Mary, whom we see praying in the upper room, is thus longer than that of the others gathered there: Mary "goes before them," "leads the way" for them.[61] *The moment of Pentecost* in Jerusalem had been prepared for by the *moment of the annunciation* in Nazareth, as well as by the cross. In the upper room Mary's journey meets the Church's journey of faith. In what way?

Among those who devoted themselves to prayer in the upper room, preparing to go "into the whole world" after receiving the Spirit, some *had been called by Jesus* gradually from the beginning of his mission in Israel. Eleven of them *had been made apostles*, and to them Jesus had passed on the mission which he himself had received from the Father. "As the Father has sent me, even so I send you" (Jn 20:21), he had said to the apostles after the resurrection. And forty days later, before returning to the Father, he had added: "when the Holy Spirit has come upon you ... *you shall be my witnesses* ... to the end of the earth" (cf. Acts 1:8). This mission of the apostles began the moment they left the upper room in Jerusalem. The Church is born and then grows through the testimony that Peter and the apostles bear to the crucified and risen Christ (cf. Acts 2:31–34; 3:15–18; 4:10–12; 5:30–32).

Mary did not directly receive this apostolic mission. She was not among those whom Jesus sent "to the whole world to teach all nations" (cf. Mt 28:19) when he conferred this mission on them. But she was in the upper room, where the apostles were preparing to take up this mission with the coming of the Spirit of Truth; she was present with them. In their midst Mary was "devoted to prayer" as the "mother of Jesus" (cf. Acts 1:13–14), of the crucified and risen Christ. And that first group of those who in faith looked "upon Jesus as the author of salvation,"[62] knew that Jesus was the Son of Mary, and that she was his Mother, and that as such she was from the moment of his conception and birth a unique witness to *the mystery of Jesus*, that mystery which before their eyes had been disclosed and confirmed in the cross and resurrection. Thus, from the very first moment, the Church "looked at" Mary through Jesus, just as she "looked at" Jesus through Mary. For the Church of that time and of every time Mary is a singular witness to the years of Jesus' infancy and hidden life at Nazareth, when she "kept all these things, pondering them in her heart" (Lk 2:19; cf. Lk 2:51).

But above all, in the Church of that time and of every time Mary was and is the one who is "blessed because she believed"; *she was the first to believe*. From the moment of the annunciation and conception, from the moment of his birth in the stable at Bethlehem, Mary followed Jesus step by step in her maternal pilgrimage of faith. She followed him during the years of his hidden life at Nazareth; she followed him also during the time after he left home, when he began "to do and to teach" (cf. Acts 1:1) in the midst of Israel. Above all she followed him in the tragic experience of Golgotha. Now, while Mary was with the apostles in the upper room in Jerusalem at the dawn of the Church, *her faith, born from the words of the annunciation, found confirmation*. The angel had said to her then: "You will conceive in your womb and bear a son, and you shall call his name Jesus. He will be great . . . and he will reign over the house of Jacob forever; and of his kingdom there will be no end." The recent events on Calvary had shrouded that promise in darkness, yet not even beneath the cross did Mary's faith fail. She had still remained the one who, like Abraham, "in hope believed against hope" (Rom 4:18). But it was only after the resurrection that hope had shown its true face and *the promise had begun to be transformed into reality*. For Jesus, before returning to the Father, had said to the apostles: "Go therefore and make disciples of all nations . . . lo, I am with you always, to the close of the age" (cf. Mt 28:19–20). Thus had spoken the one who by his resurrection had revealed himself as the conqueror of death, as the one who possessed the kingdom of which, as the angel said, "there will be no end."

27. Now, at the first dawn of the Church, at the beginning of the long journey through faith which began at Pentecost in Jerusalem, Mary was with all those who were the seed of the "new Israel." She was present among them as an exceptional witness to the mystery of Christ. And the Church was assiduous in prayer together with her, and at the same time *"contemplated her in the light of the Word made man."* It was always to be so. For when the Church "enters more intimately into the supreme mystery of the Incarnation," she thinks of the Mother of Christ with profound reverence and devotion.[63] Mary belongs indissolubly to the mystery of Christ, and she belongs also to the mystery of the Church from the beginning, from the day of the Church's birth. At the basis of what the Church has been from the beginning, and of what she must continually become from generation to generation, in the midst of all the nations of the earth, we find the one "who believed that there would be a fulfillment of what was spoken to her from the Lord" (Lk 1:45). It is precisely Mary's faith which marks the beginning of the new and eternal Covenant of God with man in Jesus Christ; this heroic *faith* of hers *"precedes"* the apostolic witness of the Church, and ever remains in the Church's heart, hidden like a special heritage of God's revelation. All those who from generation to generation accept the apostolic witness of the Church share in that mysterious inheritance, and *in a sense share in Mary's faith.*

Elizabeth's words "Blessed is she who believed" continue to accompany the Virgin also at Pentecost; they accompany her from age to age, wherever knowledge of Christ's salvific mystery spreads, through the Church's apostolic witness and service. Thus is fulfilled the prophecy of the Magnificat: "*All generations will call me blessed*; for he who is mighty has done great things for me, and holy is his name" (Lk 1:48–49). For knowledge of the mystery of Christ leads us to bless his Mother, in the form of special veneration for the *Theotókos*. But this veneration always includes a blessing of her faith, for the Virgin of Nazareth became blessed above all through this faith, in accordance with Elizabeth's words. Those who from generation to generation among the different peoples and nations of the earth accept with faith the mystery of Christ, the incarnate Word and Redeemer of the world, not only turn with veneration to Mary and confidently have recourse to her as his Mother, but also *seek in her faith support for their own*. And it is precisely this lively sharing in Mary's faith that determines her special place in the Church's pilgrimage as the new People of God throughout the earth.

28. As the Council says, "Mary figured profoundly in the history of salvation. . . . Hence when she is being preached and venerated, she summons the faithful to her Son and his sacrifice, and to love for the Father."[64] For this reason, Mary's faith, according to the Church's apostolic witness, in some way continues to become the faith of the pilgrim People of God: the faith of individuals and communities, of places and gatherings, and of the various groups existing in the Church. It is a faith that is passed on simultaneously through both the mind and the heart. It is gained or regained continually through prayer. Therefore, "*the Church* in her apostolic work also *rightly looks to her, who brought forth Christ*, conceived of the Holy Spirit and born of the Virgin, so that through the

Church Christ *may be born and may increase in the hearts of the faithful also.*"[65]

Today, as on this pilgrimage of faith we draw near to the end of the second Christian millennium, the Church, through the teaching of the Second Vatican Council, calls our attention to her vision of herself, as the "one People of God . . . among all the nations of the earth." And she reminds us of that truth according to which all the faithful, though "scattered throughout the world, are in communion with each other in the Holy Spirit."[66] We can therefore say that in this union the mystery of Pentecost is continually being accomplished. At the same time, the Lord's apostles and disciples, in all the nations of the earth, "devote themselves to prayer *together with Mary, the mother of Jesus*" (Acts 1:14). As they constitute from generation to generation the "sign of the kingdom" which is not of his world,[67] they are also aware that in the midst of this world they must *gather around that King* to whom the nations have been given in heritage (cf. Ps 2:8), to whom the Father has given "the throne of David his father," so that he "will reign over the house of Jacob for ever, and of his kingdom there will be no end."

During this time of vigil, Mary, through the same faith which made her blessed, especially from the moment of the annunciation, is *present* in the Church's mission, *present* in the Church's work of introducing into the world *the kingdom of her Son.*[68]

This presence of Mary finds many different expressions in our day, just as it did throughout the Church's history. It also has a wide field of action: through the faith and piety of individual believers; through the traditions of Christian families or "domestic churches," of parish and missionary communities, religious institutes and dioceses; through the radiance and attraction of the great shrines where not only individuals or local groups, but sometimes whole nations and societies, even whole continents, seek to meet the Mother of the Lord, the one who is blessed because she believed, is the first among believers and therefore became the Mother of Emmanuel. This is the message of the land of Palestine, the spiritual homeland of all Christians because it was the homeland of the Savior of the world and of his Mother. This is the message of the many churches in Rome and throughout the world which have been raised up in the course of the centuries by the faith of Christians. This is the message of centers like Guadalupe, Lourdes, Fatima, and the others situated in the various countries. Among them how could I fail to mention the one in my own native land, Jasna Gora? One could perhaps speak of a specific "geography" of faith and Marian devotion, which includes all these special places of pilgrimage where the People of God seek to meet the Mother of God in order to find, within the radius of the maternal presence of her, "who believed," a strengthening of their own faith. For *in Mary's faith*, first at the annunciation and then fully at the foot of the cross, an *interior space* was reopened within humanity which the eternal Father can fill "with every spiritual blessing." It is the space "of the new and eternal Covenant,"[69] and it continues to exist in the Church, which in Christ is "a kind of sacrament or sign of intimate union with God, and of the unity of all mankind."[70]

In the faith which Mary professed at the annunciation as the "handmaid of the Lord" and in which she constantly "precedes" the pilgrim People of God throughout the earth, the *Church* "*strives* energetically and constantly *to bring all humanity . . . back to Christ its Head* in the unity of his Spirit."[71]

The Church's journey and the unity of all Christians

29. "In all of Christ's disciples the Spirit arouses the desire to be peacefully *united,* in the manner determined by Christ, as one flock *under one shepherd.*"[72] The journey of the Church, especially in our own time, is marked by the sign of ecumenism: Christians are seeking ways to restore that unity which Christ implored from the Father for his disciples on the day before his passion: "*That they may all be one*; even as you, Father, are in me, and I in you, that they also may be in us, so that the world *may believe* that you have sent me" (Jn 17:21). The unity of Christ's disciples, therefore, is a great sign given in order to kindle faith in the world while their division constitutes a scandal.[73]

The ecumenical movement, on the basis of a clearer and more widespread awareness of the urgent need to achieve the unity of all Christians, has found on the part of the Catholic Church its culminating expression in the work of the Second Vatican Council: Christians must deepen in themselves and each of their communities that "obedience of faith" of which Mary is the first and brightest example. And since she "shines forth on earth . . . as a sign of sure hope and solace for the pilgrim People of God," "it gives great joy and comfort to this most holy Synod that *among the divided brethren*, too, there are those who give due honor to the Mother of our Lord and Savior. This is especially so among the Easterners."[74]

30. Christians know that their unity will be truly rediscovered only if it is based on the unity of their faith. They must resolve considerable discrepancies of doctrine concerning the mystery and ministry of the Church, and sometimes also concerning the role of Mary in the work of salvation.[75] The dialogues begun by the Catholic Church with the Churches and ecclesial communities of the West[76] are steadily converging upon these *two inseparable aspects* of the same mystery of salvation. If the mystery of the Word made flesh enables us to glimpse the mystery of the divine motherhood and if, in turn, contemplation of the Mother of God brings us to a more profound understanding of the mystery of the Incarnation, then the same must be said for the mystery of the Church and Mary's role in the work of salvation. By a more profound study of both Mary and the Church, clarifying each by the light of the other, Christians who are eager to do what Jesus tells them—as their Mother recommends (cf. Jn 2:5)—will be able to go forward together on this "pilgrimage of faith." Mary, who is still the model of this pilgrimage, is to lead them to the unity which is willed by their one Lord and so much desired by those who are attentively listening to what "the Spirit is saying to the Churches" today (Rev 2:7, 11, 17).

Meanwhile, it is a hopeful sign that these Churches and ecclesial communities are finding agreement with the Catholic Church on fundamental points of Christian belief, including matters relating to the Virgin Mary. For they recognize her as the Mother of the Lord and hold that this forms part of our faith in Christ, true God and true man. They look to her who at the foot of the cross accepts as her son the beloved disciple, the one who in his turn accepts her as his mother.

Therefore, why should we not all together look to her as *our common Mother*, who prays for the unity of God's family and who "precedes" us all at the head of the long line of witnesses of faith in the one Lord, the Son of God, who was conceived in her virginal womb by the power of the Holy Spirit?

31. On the other hand, I wish to emphasize how profoundly the Catholic Church, the Orthodox Church, and the ancient Churches of the East feel united by love and praise of the *Theotókos*. Not only "basic dogmas of the Christian faith concerning the Trinity and God's Word made flesh of the Virgin Mary were defined in ecumenical councils held in the East,"[77] but also in their liturgical worship "the Orientals pay high tribute, in very beautiful hymns, to Mary ever Virgin ... God's Most Holy Mother."[78]

The brethren of these Churches have experienced a complex history, but it is one that has always been marked by an intense desire for Christian commitment and apostolic activity, despite frequent persecution, even to the point of bloodshed. It is a history of fidelity to the Lord, an authentic "pilgrimage of faith" in space and time, during which Eastern Christians have always looked with boundless trust to the Mother of the Lord, celebrated her with praise, and invoked her with unceasing prayer. In the difficult moments of their troubled Christian existence, "they have taken refuge under her protection,"[79] conscious of having in her a powerful aid. The Churches which profess the doctrine of Ephesus proclaim the Virgin as "true Mother of God," since "our Lord Jesus Christ, born of the Father before time began according to his divinity, in the last days, for our sake and for our salvation, was himself begotten of Mary, the Virgin Mother of God according to his humanity."[80] The Greek Fathers and the Byzantine tradition, contemplating the Virgin in the light of the Word made flesh, have sought to penetrate the depth of that bond which unites Mary, as the Mother of God, to Christ and the Church: the Virgin is a permanent presence in the whole reality of the salvific mystery.

The Coptic and Ethiopian traditions were introduced to this contemplation of the mystery of Mary by St. Cyril of Alexandria, and in their turn they have celebrated it with a profuse poetic blossoming.[81] The poetic genius of St. Ephrem the Syrian, called "the lyre of the Holy Spirit," tirelessly sang of Mary, leaving a still living mark on the whole tradition of the Syriac Church.[82]

In his panegyric of the *Theotókos*, St. Gregory of Narek, one of the outstanding glories of Armenia, with powerful poetic inspiration ponders the different aspects of the mystery of the Incarnation, and each of them is for him an occasion to sing and extol the extraordinary dignity and magnificent beauty of the Virgin Mary, Mother of the Word made flesh.[83]

It does not surprise us therefore that Mary occupies a privileged place in the worship of the ancient Oriental

Churches with an incomparable abundance of feasts and hymns.

32. In the Byzantine liturgy, in all the hours of the divine office, praise of the Mother is linked with praise of her Son and with the praise which, through the Son, is offered up to the Father in the Holy Spirit. In the Anaphora or Eucharistic Prayer of St. John Chrysostom, immediately after the epiclesis the assembled community sings in honor of the Mother of God: "It is truly just to proclaim you blessed, O Mother of God, who are most blessed, all pure, and Mother of our God. We magnify you who are more honorable than the cherubim and incomparably more glorious than the seraphim, you who, without losing your virginity, gave birth to the Word of God, you who are truly the Mother of God."

These praises, which in every celebration of the Eucharistic liturgy are offered to Mary, have molded the faith, piety, and prayer of the faithful. In the course of the centuries they have permeated their whole spiritual outlook, fostering in them a profound devotion to the "All Holy Mother of God."

33. This year there occurs the twelfth centenary of the Second Ecumenical Council of Nicaea (787). Putting an end to the well-known controversy about the cult of sacred images, this council defined that, according to the teaching of the holy Fathers and the universal tradition of the Church, there could be exposed for the veneration of the faithful, together with the cross, also images of the Mother of God, of the angels, and of the saints, in churches and houses and at the roadside.[84] This custom has been maintained in the whole of the East and also in the West. Images of the Virgin have a place of honor in

churches and houses. In them Mary is represented in a number of ways: as the throne of God carrying the Lord and giving him to humanity (*Theotókos*); as the way that leads to Christ and manifests him (*Hodegetria*); as a praying figure in an attitude of intercession and as a sign of the divine presence on the journey of the faithful until the day of the Lord (*Deësis*); as the protectress who stretches out her mantle over the peoples *(Pokrov),* or as the merciful Virgin of tenderness (*Eleousa*). She is usually represented with her Son, the child Jesus, in her arms: it is the relationship with the Son which glorifies the Mother. Sometimes she embraces him with tenderness (*Glykophilousa*); at other times she is a hieratic figure, apparently rapt in contemplation of him, who is the Lord of history (cf. Rev 5:9–14).[85]

It is also appropriate to mention the icon of Our Lady of Vladimir, which continually accompanied the pilgrimage of faith of the peoples of ancient Rus'. The first millennium of the conversion of those noble lands to Christianity is approaching: lands of humble folk, of thinkers and of saints. The icons are still venerated in the Ukraine, in Byelorussia and in Russia under various titles. They are images which witness to the faith and spirit of prayer of that people, who sense the presence and protection of the Mother of God. In these icons the Virgin shines as the image of divine beauty, the abode of Eternal Wisdom, the figure of the one who prays, the prototype of contemplation, the image of glory: she who even in her earthly life possessed the spiritual knowledge inaccessible to human reasoning and who attained through faith the most sublime knowledge. I also recall the icon of the Virgin of the Cenacle, praying with the apostles as they awaited the Holy Spirit: could she not become the sign of hope for all those who, in fraternal dialogue, wish to deepen their obedience of faith?

34. Such a wealth of praise, built up by the different forms of the Church's great tradition, could help us to hasten the day when the Church can begin once more to breathe fully with her "two lungs," the East and the West. As I have often said, this is more than ever necessary today. It would be an effective aid in furthering the progress of the dialogue already taking place between the Catholic Church and the Churches and ecclesial communities of the West.[86] It would also be the way for the pilgrim Church to sing and to live more perfectly her "Magnificat."

The "Magnificat" of the pilgrim Church

35. At the present stage of her journey, therefore, the Church seeks to rediscover the unity of all who profess their faith in Christ, in order to show obedience to her Lord, who prayed for this unity before his passion. "Like a pilgrim in a foreign land, the Church presses forward amid the persecutions of the world and the consolations of God, announcing the cross and death of the Lord until he comes."[87] "Moving forward through trial and tribulation, *the Church is strengthened by the power of God's grace promised to her by the Lord,* so that in the weakness of the flesh she may not waver from perfect fidelity, but remain a bride worthy of her Lord; that moved by the Holy Spirit she may never cease to renew herself, until

through the cross she arrives at the light which knows no setting."[88]

The Virgin Mother is constantly present on this journey of faith of the People of God toward the light. This is shown in a special way by *the canticle of the "Magnificat," which, having welled up from the depths of Mary's faith* at the visitation, ceaselessly re-echoes in the heart of the Church down the centuries. This is proved by its daily recitation in the liturgy of Vespers and at many other moments of both personal and communal devotion.

"My soul magnifies the Lord,
    and my spirit rejoices in God my Savior,
for he has looked on his servant in her lowliness.
    For behold, henceforth all generations will call me
        blessed;
for he who is mighty has done great things for me,
    and holy is his name:
And his mercy is from age to age
    on those who fear him.
He has shown strength with his arm,
    he has scattered the proudhearted,
he has cast down the mighty from their thrones,
    and lifted up the lowly;
he has filled the hungry with good things,
    sent the rich away empty.
He has helped his servant Israel,
    remembering his mercy,
as he spoke to our fathers,

to Abraham and to his posterity forever."
(Lk 1:46–55)

36. When Elizabeth greeted her young kinswoman coming from Nazareth, *Mary replied with the Magnificat*. In her greeting, Elizabeth first called Mary "blessed" because of "the fruit of her womb," and then she called her "blessed" because of her faith (cf. Lk 1:42, 45). These two blessings referred directly to the annunciation. Now, at the visitation, when Elizabeth's greeting bears witness to that culminating moment, Mary's faith acquires a new consciousness and a new expression. That which remained hidden in the depths of the "obedience of faith" at the annunciation can now be said to spring forth like a clear and lifegiving flame of the spirit. The words used by Mary on the threshold of Elizabeth's house are *an inspired profession of her faith*, in which *her response to the revealed word* is expressed with the religious and poetical exultation of her whole being toward God. In these sublime words, which are simultaneously very simple and wholly inspired by the sacred texts of the people of Israel,[89] Mary's personal experience, the ecstasy of her heart, shines forth. In them shines a ray of the mystery of God, the glory of his ineffable holiness, the eternal *love which, as an irrevocable gift, enters into human history.*

Mary is the first to share in this new revelation of God and, within the same, in this new "self-giving" of God. Therefore she proclaims: "For he who is mighty has done great things for me, and holy is his name." Her words reflect a joy of spirit which is difficult to express: "My spirit rejoices in God my Savior." Indeed, "the deepest truth about God and the salvation of man is made clear to us in Christ, who is at the same time the mediator and the fullness of all revelation."[90] In her exultation Mary confesses that she finds herself *in the very heart of this fullness* of Christ. She is conscious that the promise made to the fathers, first of all "to Abraham and to his posterity forever," is being fulfilled in herself. She is thus aware that concentrated within herself as the mother of Christ is *the whole salvific economy*, in which "from age to age" is manifested he who as the God of the Covenant, "remembers his mercy."

37. The Church, which from the beginning has modeled her earthly journey on that of the Mother of God, constantly repeats after her the words of the Magnificat. From the depths of the Virgin's faith at the annunciation and the visitation, the Church derives the truth about the God of the Covenant: the God who is Almighty and does "great things" for man: "holy is his name." In the Magnificat the Church sees uprooted that sin which is found at the outset of the earthly history of man and woman, the sin of disbelief and of "little faith" in God. In contrast with the "suspicion" which the "father of lies" sowed in the heart of Eve the first woman, Mary, whom tradition is wont to call the "new Eve"[91] and the true "Mother of the living,"[92] boldly proclaims the *undimmed* truth about God: the holy and almighty God, who from the beginning is *the source of all gifts*, he who "has done great things" in her, as well as in the whole universe. In the act of creation God gives existence to all that is. In creating man, God gives him the dignity of the image and likeness of himself in a special way as compared with all earthly creatures. Moreover, in his desire to give, *God*

gives himself in the Son, notwithstanding man's sin: "He so loved the world that he gave his only Son" (Jn 3:16). Mary is the first witness of this marvelous truth, which will be fully accomplished through "the works and words" (cf. Acts 1:1) of her Son and definitively through his cross and resurrection.

The Church, which even "amid trials and tribulations" does not cease repeating with Mary the words of the Magnificat, is sustained by the power of God's truth, proclaimed on that occasion with such extraordinary simplicity. At the same time, *by means of this truth about God*, the Church *desires to shed light upon* the difficult and sometimes tangled paths of man's earthly existence. The Church's journey, therefore, near the end of the second Christian millennium, involves a renewed commitment to her mission. Following him who said of himself: "[God] has anointed me *to preach good news to the poor*" (cf. Lk 4:18), the Church has sought from generation to generation and still seeks today to accomplish that same mission.

The Church's *love of preference for the poor* is wonderfully inscribed in Mary's Magnificat. The God of the Covenant, celebrated in the exultation of her spirit by the Virgin of Nazareth, is also he who "has cast down the mighty from their thrones, and lifted up the lowly . . . filled the hungry with good things, sent the rich away empty . . . scattered the proud hearted . . . and his mercy is from age to age on those who fear him." Mary is deeply imbued with the spirit of the "poor of Yahweh," who in the prayer of the psalms awaited from God their salvation, placing all their trust in him (cf. Ps 25; 31; 35; 55). Mary truly proclaims the coming of the "messiah of the poor" (cf. Is 11:4; 61:1). Drawing from Mary's heart, from the depth of her faith expressed in the words of the Magnificat, the Church renews ever more effectively in herself the awareness that *the truth about God who saves*, the truth about God who is the source of every gift, *cannot be separated from the manifestation of his love of preference for the poor and humble*, that love which, celebrated in the Magnificat, is later expressed in the words and works of Jesus.

The Church is thus aware—and at the present time this awareness is particularly vivid—not only that these two elements of the message contained in the Magnificat cannot be separated, but also that there is a duty to safeguard carefully the importance of "the poor" and of "the option in favor of the poor" in the word of the living God. These are matters and questions intimately connected with the *Christian meaning of freedom and liberation*. "Mary is totally dependent upon God and completely directed toward him, and at the side of her Son, she is *the most perfect image of freedom and of the liberation* of humanity and of the universe. It is to her as Mother and Model that the Church must look in order to understand in its completeness the meaning of her own mission."[93]

PONDER

Mary, the woman, was among the first to be called specifically to serve and follow Christ, then others came from whom the Lord selected twelve. Our Holy Father spends many paragraphs convincing us of when and how the Church came into existence. He focuses on its *inner* pilgrimage—the *embodiment* of Christ. John Paul II also wants to convince us that the Marian response came before the Petrine authority. Doesn't reading Sacred Scripture show that there were many believers before Christ set up leadership? Clearly, we are called to have faith like Mary did. It is out of this loving faith that Mary responds and serves. Our faith, which calls for a loving response, is the true leadership of the Church.

Through the centuries, the Church actually continues, shares in, learns from, and loves Mary's faith. That's what *devotion* to her has been. We simply cannot forget Mary's faith. We admire and share that holy faith, or we don't. From John Paul II's papal perspective, the Church unites all minds in truth and all hearts in love—in Christ Jesus! He encourages us to seek the commonalities, to respect, value, and admire the differences—and sort them out, if that is possible.

For you and me, the Church is probably our neighbors down the street, who can be so irritating. One wipes his nose on the back of his hand, then offers it in peace. Another complains and gossips while flipping pancakes at a parish function to feed the poor. Yet somehow, as long as Christ the Redeemer is central, all is well. Mary knows it; she is the first and greatest believer; she is actively present—even now. She continues to tell all of us, "Do whatever he tells you" (Jn 2:5).

1. What does John Paul II mean when he says, "For *in Mary's faith*, first at the annunciation and then fully at the foot of the cross, an *interior space* was reopened

within humanity which the eternal Father can fill 'with every spiritual blessing.' It is the space 'of the new and eternal Covenant,' and it continues to exist in the Church, which in Christ is 'a kind of sacrament or sign of intimate union with God, and of the unity of all mankind'" (LG, 1) (par. 28)?

2. Mary teaches, "Do whatever he tells you." What if the servants hadn't listened to her? What if no one seems to listen to *your* faith story (par. 26)?

3. John Paul's use of the phrase "geography of faith" in this document popularized the term so that it became a type of catchphrase. What did the Holy Father mean when he used that expression (par. 28)?

4. John Paul II talks about "Mary's personal experience, the ecstasy of her heart" (par. 36) as sung in the Magnificat, an experience that formed her through and through. Our personal experiences, too, form us. They can turn us sour, causing us to linger on the dark side of things, but we can also use our will to examine God's infinite goodness and blessings, which might ultimately show up in that dark place. As the pope writes, can there shine in that darkness "a ray of the mystery of God, the glory of his ineffable holiness, the eternal *love, which, as an irrevocable gift,*" *enters also into our own personal history* (par. 38)? Isn't it my choice to search for the mysterious reason of eternal love, or do I turn away, lost in the dark places?

Pray

Mary, as I read the teachings of our beloved John Paul II spoken to us long ago, they seem as fresh as today. I wonder about him and about you. How could he know all that about your faith, your way of living, and your reactions to God? Is it just our imagination that places all these marvelous thoughts in our minds? Some of my neighbors think so. I find it so difficult to share the joyous peace-giving moments that pondering your life gives me.

Yet, when I ask you to be with me, show yourself gentle and powerful in my life, and help me, I truly believe that I am speaking to you and you hear me. Do I believe this because someone told me it is so?

Mary, you are part of the treasure of faith that Scripture gives us. I want to be immersed in your experiences so that my life finds some of the richness and meaning that yours had. But how? There is that ancient saying: One learns to walk by walking, and to love by loving. Talking about prayer is not necessarily prayer. Will my magnificats ever be like yours?

Act

Savor the Magnificat as the Church does. Teach yourself to pray spontaneously and joyfully like Mary.

Part III

Maternal Mediation

Mary, the Handmaid of the Lord

38. The Church knows and teaches with St. Paul that *there is only one mediator*: "For there is one God, and there is one mediator between God and men, the man Christ Jesus, who gave himself as a ransom for all" (1 Tm 2:5–6). "The maternal role of Mary toward people in no way obscures or diminishes the unique mediation of Christ, but rather shows its power":[94] it is mediation in Christ.

The Church knows and teaches that "all *the saving influences of the Blessed Virgin* on mankind originate . . . from the divine pleasure. They flow forth *from the superabundance of the merits of Christ*, rest on his mediation, depend entirely on it, and draw all their power from it. In no way do they impede the immediate union of the faithful with Christ. Rather, they foster this union."[95] This saving influence is sustained by the Holy Spirit, who, just as he overshadowed the Virgin Mary when he began in her the divine motherhood, in a similar way constantly sustains her solicitude for the brothers and sisters of her Son.

In effect, Mary's mediation *is intimately linked with her motherhood*. It possesses a specifically maternal character, which distinguishes it from the mediation of the other creatures who in various and always subordinate ways share in the one mediation of Christ, although her own mediation is also a shared mediation.[96] In fact, while it is true that "no creature could ever be classed with the incarnate Word and Redeemer," at the same time "the unique mediation of the Redeemer does not exclude but rather gives rise among creatures to *a manifold cooperation* which is but a sharing in this unique source." And thus "the one goodness of God is in reality communicated diversely to his creatures."[97]

The teaching of the Second Vatican Council presents the truth of Mary's mediation as *"a sharing in the one unique source that is the mediation of Christ himself."* Thus we read: "The Church does not hesitate to profess this subordinate role of Mary. She experiences it continuously and commends it to the hearts of the faithful, so that, encouraged by this maternal help, they may more closely adhere to the Mediator and Redeemer."[98] This role is at the same time *special and extraordinary*. It flows from her divine motherhood and can be understood and lived in faith only on the basis of the full truth of this motherhood. Since by virtue of divine election Mary is the earthly Mother of the Father's consubstantial Son and his "generous companion" in the work of redemption, "she is a mother to us in the order of grace."[99] This role constitutes a real dimension of her presence in the saving mystery of Christ and the Church.

39. From this point of view we must consider once more the fundamental event in the economy of salvation, namely the Incarnation of the Word at the moment of the annunciation. It is significant that Mary, recognizing in the words of the divine messenger the will of the Most High and submitting to his power, says: "*Behold, I am the handmaid* of the Lord; let it be to me according to your word" (Lk 1:38). The first moment of submission to the one mediation "between God and men"—the mediation of Jesus Christ—is the Virgin of Nazareth's acceptance of motherhood. Mary consents to God's choice, in order to become through the power of the Holy Spirit the Mother of the Son of God. It can be said that a *consent to motherhood* is above all *a result of her total self-giving to God in virginity*. Mary accepted her election as Mother of the Son of God, guided by spousal love, the love which totally "consecrates" a human being to God. By virtue of this love, Mary wished to be always and in all things "given to God," living in virginity. The words "Behold, I am the handmaid of the Lord" express the fact that from the outset she accepted and understood her own motherhood as a total *gift of self*, a gift of her person to the service of the saving plans of the Most High. And to the very end she lived her entire maternal sharing in the life of Jesus Christ, her Son, in a way that matched her vocation to virginity.

Mary's motherhood, completely pervaded by her spousal attitude as the "handmaid of the Lord," constitutes the first and fundamental dimension of that mediation which the Church confesses and proclaims in her regard [100] and continually "commends to the hearts of the faithful," since the Church has great trust in her. For it must be recognized that before anyone else it was God himself, the Eternal Father, who *entrusted himself to the Virgin of Nazareth*, giving her his own Son in the mystery of the Incarnation. Her election to the supreme office and dignity of Mother of the Son of God refers, on the ontological level, to the very reality of the union of the two natures in the person of the Word (*hypostatic union*). This basic fact of being the Mother of the Son of God is from the very beginning a complete openness to the person of Christ, to his whole work, to his whole mission. The words "Behold, I am the handmaid of the Lord" testify to Mary's openness of spirit: she perfectly unites in herself the love proper to virginity and the love characteristic of motherhood, which are joined and, as it were, fused together.

For this reason Mary became not only the "nursing mother" of the Son of Man but also the "associate of unique nobility"[101] of the messiah and Redeemer. As I have already said, she advanced in her pilgrimage of faith, and in this *pilgrimage* to the foot of the cross there was simultaneously accomplished her maternal *cooperation* with the Savior's whole mission through her actions and sufferings. Along the path of this collaboration with the work of her Son, the Redeemer, Mary's motherhood itself underwent a singular transformation, becoming ever more imbued with "burning charity" toward all those to whom Christ's mission was directed. Through this "burning charity," which sought to achieve, in union with Christ, the restoration of "supernatural life to souls,"[102] Mary *entered, in a way all her own, into the one mediation* "between God and men" *which is the mediation of the man Christ Jesus.* If she was the first to experience within herself the supernatural consequences of this one mediation—in the annunciation she had been greeted as "full of grace"—then we must say that through this fullness of grace and supernatural life she was especially predisposed to cooperation with Christ, the one Mediator of human salvation. *And such cooperation* is *precisely this mediation subordinated* to the mediation of Christ.

In Mary's case we have a special and exceptional mediation, based upon her "fullness of grace," which was expressed in the complete willingness of the "handmaid of the Lord." In response to this interior willingness of his Mother, *Jesus Christ prepared her* ever more completely to become for all people their "mother in the order of grace." This is indicated, at least indirectly, by certain details noted by the synoptics (cf. Lk 11:28; 8:20–21; Mk 3:32–35; Mt 12:47–50) and still more so by the Gospel of John (cf. 2:1–12; 19:25–27), which I have already mentioned. Particularly eloquent in this regard are the words spoken by Jesus on the cross to Mary and John.

40. After the events of the resurrection and ascension Mary entered the upper room together with the apostles to await Pentecost, and was present there as the Mother of the glorified Lord. She was not only the one who "advanced in her pilgrimage of faith" and loyally persevered in her union with her Son "unto the cross," *but she was also the "handmaid of the Lord," left by her Son as Mother in the midst of the infant Church:* "Behold your mother." Thus there began to develop a special bond between this Mother and the Church. For the infant

Church was the fruit of the cross and resurrection of her Son. Mary, who from the beginning had given herself without reserve to the person and work of her Son, could not but pour out upon the Church, from the very beginning, her maternal self-giving. After her Son's departure, her motherhood remains in the Church as maternal mediation: interceding for all her children, the Mother cooperates in the saving work of her Son, the Redeemer of the world. In fact the Council teaches that the "motherhood of Mary in the order of grace . . . *will last without interruption* until the eternal fulfillment of all the elect."[103] With the redeeming death of her Son, the maternal mediation of the handmaid of the Lord took on a universal dimension, for the work of redemption embraces the whole of humanity. Thus there is manifested in a singular way the efficacy of the one and universal mediation of Christ "between God and men." Mary's cooperation shares, in its subordinate character, *in the universality of the mediation of the Redeemer*, the one Mediator. This is clearly indicated by the Council in the words quoted above.

"For," the text goes on, "taken up to heaven, she did not lay aside this saving role, but by her manifold acts of intercession continues to win for us gifts of eternal salvation."[104] With this character of "intercession," first manifested at Cana in Galilee, Mary's mediation continues in the history of the Church and the world. We read that Mary "by her maternal charity, cares for the brethren of her Son who still journey on earth surrounded by dangers and difficulties, until they are led to their happy homeland."[105] In this way Mary's motherhood continues unceasingly in the Church as the mediation that intercedes, and the Church expresses her faith in this truth by invoking Mary "under the titles of Advocate, Auxiliatrix, Adjutrix and Mediatrix."[106]

41. Through her mediation, subordinate to that of the Redeemer, Mary contributes *in a special way to the union of the pilgrim Church* on earth with the eschatological and heavenly *reality* of the communion of saints, since she has already been "assumed into heaven."[107] The truth of the Assumption, defined by Pius XII, is reaffirmed by the Second Vatican Council, which thus expresses the Church's faith: "Preserved free from all guilt of original sin, the immaculate Virgin *was taken up body and soul into heavenly glory* upon the completion of her earthly sojourn. She was *exalted* by the Lord *as Queen of the Universe*, in order that she might be the more thoroughly conformed to her Son, the Lord of lords (cf. Rev 19:16) and the conqueror of sin and death."[108] In this teaching Pius XII was in continuity with Tradition, which has found many different expressions in the history of the Church, both in the East and in the West.

By the mystery of the Assumption into heaven there were definitively accomplished in Mary all the effects of the one mediation of *Christ the Redeemer of the world* and *risen Lord:* "In Christ shall all be made alive, but each in his own order: Christ the first fruits, then at his coming those who belong to Christ" (1 Cor 15:22–23). In the mystery of the Assumption is expressed the faith of the Church, according to which Mary is "united by a close and indissoluble bond" to Christ, for, if as Virgin and Mother she was singularly united with him *in his first coming*, so through her continued collaboration with him she will also be united with him in expectation of the second; "redeemed in an especially sublime manner by reason of the merits of her Son,"[109] she also has that specifically maternal role of mediatrix of mercy *at his final coming*, when all those who belong to Christ "shall be made alive," when "the last enemy to be destroyed is death" (1 Cor 15:26).[110]

Connected with this exaltation of the noble "Daughter of Zion"[111] through her Assumption into heaven is the mystery of her eternal glory. For the Mother of Christ is glorified as "Queen of the Universe."[112] She who at the annunciation called herself the "handmaid of the Lord" remained throughout her earthly life faithful to what this name expresses. In this she confirmed that she was a true "disciple" of Christ, who strongly emphasized that his mission was one of service: "the Son of Man came not to be served but to serve, and to give his life as a ransom for many" (Mt 20:28). In this way Mary became the first of those who, "serving Christ also in others, with humility and patience lead their brothers and sisters to that King whom to serve is to reign,"[113] and she fully obtained that "state of royal freedom" proper to Christ's disciples: to serve means to reign!

"Christ obeyed even at the cost of death, and was therefore raised up by the Father (cf. Phil 2:8–9). Thus he entered into the glory of his kingdom. To him all things are made subject until he subjects himself and all created things to the Father, that God may be all in all (cf. 1 Cor 15:27–28)."[114] Mary, the handmaid of the Lord, has a share in this kingdom of the Son.[115] The *glory of serving* does not cease to be her royal exaltation: assumed into heaven, she does not cease her saving service, which expresses her maternal mediation "until the eternal fulfillment of all the elect."[116] Thus, she who here on earth "loyally persevered in her union with her Son unto the cross," continues to remain united with him, while now *all things are subjected to him, until he subjects to the Father himself and all things."* Thus in her Assumption into heaven, Mary is as it were clothed by the whole reality of the communion of saints, and her very union with the Son in glory is wholly oriented toward the definitive fullness of the kingdom, *when "God will be all in all."*

In this phase too Mary's maternal mediation does not cease to be subordinate to him who is the one Mediator, *until the final realization of "the fullness of time,"* that is to say until "all things are united in Christ" (cf. Eph 1:10).

Mary in the life of the Church and of every Christian

42. Linking itself with Tradition, the Second Vatican Council brought new light to bear on the role of the Mother of Christ in the life of the Church. "Through the gift . . . of divine motherhood, Mary is united with her Son, the Redeemer, and with his singular graces and offices. By these, the Blessed Virgin is also intimately united with the Church: *the Mother of God is a figure of the Church* in the matter of faith, charity, and perfect union with Christ."[117] We have already noted how, from the beginning, Mary remains with the apostles in expectation of Pentecost and how, as "the blessed one who believed," she is present in the midst of the

pilgrim Church from generation to generation through faith and as the model of the hope which does not disappoint (cf. Rom 5:5).

Mary believed in the fulfillment of what had been said to her by the Lord. As Virgin, she believed that she would conceive and bear a son: the "Holy One," who bears the name of "Son of God," the name "Jesus" (= God who saves). As handmaid of the Lord, she remained in perfect fidelity to the person and mission of this Son. As Mother, *"believing and obeying . . .* she brought forth on earth the *Father's Son.* This she did, knowing not man but overshadowed by the Holy Spirit."[118]

For these reasons Mary is honored in the Church "with special reverence. Indeed, from most ancient times the Blessed Virgin Mary has been venerated under the title of 'Godbearer.' In all perils and needs, the faithful have fled prayerfully to her protection."[119] This cult is altogether special: it bears in itself and *expresses* the profound *link* which exists *between the Mother of Christ and the Church.*[120] As Virgin and Mother, Mary remains for the Church a "permanent model." It can therefore be said that especially under this aspect, namely as a model, or rather as a "figure," Mary, present in the mystery of Christ, remains constantly present also in the mystery of the Church. For the Church too is "called mother and virgin," and these names have a profound biblical and theological justification.[121]

43. The *Church "becomes* herself *a mother* by accepting God's word with fidelity."[122] Like Mary, who first believed by accepting the Word of God revealed to her at the annunciation and by remaining faithful to that word in all her trials

even unto the cross, so too the Church becomes a mother when, *accepting with fidelity the Word of God,* "by her preaching and by Baptism *she brings forth to a new and immortal life children* who are conceived *of the Holy Spirit* and born of God."[123] This "maternal" characteristic of the Church was expressed in a particularly vivid way by the apostle to the Gentiles when he wrote: "My little children, with whom I am again in travail until Christ be formed in you!" (Gal 4:19). These words of St. Paul contain an interesting sign of the early Church's awareness of her own motherhood, linked to her apostolic service to mankind. This awareness enabled and still enables the Church to see the mystery of her life and mission modeled *upon the example of the Mother of the Son,* who is "the firstborn among many brethren" (Rom 8:29).

It can be said that from Mary the Church also learns her own motherhood: she recognizes the maternal dimension of her vocation, which is essentially bound to her sacramental nature, in "contemplating Mary's mysterious sanctity, imitating her charity, and faithfully fulfilling the Father's will."[124] If the Church is the sign and instrument of intimate union with God, she is so by reason of her motherhood, because, receiving life from the Spirit, she "generates" sons and daughters of the human race to a new life in Christ. For, just as *Mary is at the service of the mystery of the Incarnation,* so *the Church* is always *at the service of the mystery of adoption to sonship* through grace.

Likewise, following the example of Mary, the Church remains the virgin faithful to her spouse: "The Church herself is a virgin who keeps whole and pure the fidelity she has pledged to her Spouse."[125] For the Church is the spouse of Christ, as is clear from the Pauline Letters (cf. Eph 5:21–33; 2 Cor 11:2), and from the title found in John: "bride of the Lamb" (Rev 21:9). If *the Church* as spouse "keeps the fidelity she *has pledged* to Christ," this fidelity, even though in the Apostle's teaching it has become an image of marriage (cf. Eph 5:23–33), also has value as a model of total self-giving to God in celibacy "for the kingdom of heaven," *in virginity consecrated to God* (cf. Mt 19:11–12; 2 Cor 11:2). Precisely such virginity, after the example of the Virgin of Nazareth, is the source of a special spiritual fruitfulness: *it is the source of motherhood in the Holy Spirit.*

But *the Church* also preserves the faith *received from* Christ. Following the example of Mary, who kept and pondered in her heart everything relating to her divine Son (cf. Lk 2:19, 51), the Church is committed to preserving the Word of God and investigating its riches with discernment and prudence, in order to bear faithful witness to it before all mankind in every age.[126]

44. Given Mary's relationship to the Church as an exemplar, the Church is close to her and seeks to become like her: "Imitating the Mother of her Lord, and by the power of the Holy Spirit, she preserves with virginal purity an integral faith, a firm hope, and a sincere charity."[127] Mary is thus present in the mystery of the Church as a *model.* But the Church's mystery also consists in generating people to a new and immortal life: this is her motherhood in the Holy Spirit. And here Mary is not only the model and figure of the Church; she is much more. For *"with maternal love she cooperates in the birth*

and development" of the sons and daughters of Mother Church. The Church's motherhood is accomplished not only according to the model and figure of the Mother of God but also with her "cooperation." The Church *draws* abundantly from this cooperation, that is to say from the maternal mediation which is characteristic of Mary, insofar as already on earth she cooperated in the rebirth and development of the Church's sons and daughters, as the Mother of that Son whom the Father "placed as the firstborn among many brethren."[128]

She cooperated, as the Second Vatican Council teaches, with a maternal love.[129] Here we perceive the real value of the words spoken by Jesus to his Mother at the hour of the cross: "Woman, behold your son" and to the disciple: "Behold your mother" (Jn 19:26–27). They are words which determine *Mary's place in the life of Christ's disciples* and they express—as I have already said—the new motherhood of the Mother of the Redeemer: a spiritual motherhood, born from the heart of the Paschal Mystery of the Redeemer of the world. It is a motherhood in the order of grace, for it implores the gift of the Spirit, who raises up the new children of God, redeemed through the sacrifice of Christ: that Spirit whom, together with the Church, Mary too received on the day of Pentecost.

Her motherhood is particularly noted and experienced by the Christian people at the *Sacred Banquet*—the liturgical celebration of the mystery of the redemption—at which Christ, his true *body born of the Virgin Mary*, becomes present.

The piety of the Christian people has always very rightly sensed a *profound link* between devotion to the Blessed Virgin and worship of the Eucharist: this is a fact that can be seen in the liturgy of both the West and the East, in the traditions of the religious families, in the modern movements of spirituality, including those for youth, and in the pastoral practice of the Marian shrines. *Mary guides the faithful to the Eucharist.*

45. Of the essence of motherhood is the fact that it concerns the person. Motherhood always establishes a *unique and unrepeatable relationship* between two people: *between mother and child* and *between child and mother.* Even when the same woman is the mother of many children, her personal relationship with each one of them is of the very essence of motherhood. For each child is generated in a unique and unrepeatable way, and this is true both for the mother and for the child. Each child is surrounded in the same way by that maternal love on which are based the child's development and coming to maturity as a human being.

It can be said that motherhood "in the order of grace" preserves the analogy with what "in the order of nature" characterizes the union between mother and child. In the light of this fact it becomes easier to understand why in Christ's testament on Golgotha his Mother's new motherhood is expressed in the singular, in reference to one man: "Behold your son."

It can also be said that these same words fully show the reason *for the Marian dimension of the life of Christ's disciples.* This is true not only of John, who at that hour stood at the foot of the cross together with his Master's Mother, but it is also true of every disciple of Christ, of every Christian. The Redeemer entrusts his mother to the disciple, and at the same time he gives her to him as his mother. Mary's motherhood, which becomes man's inheritance, is a gift: *a gift which Christ himself makes* personally to every individual. The Redeemer entrusts Mary to John because he entrusts John to Mary. At the foot of the cross there begins that special *entrusting of humanity to the Mother of Christ*, which in the history of the Church has been practiced and expressed in different ways. The same apostle and evangelist, after reporting the words addressed by Jesus on the cross to his Mother and to himself, adds: "And from that hour the disciple took her to his own home" (Jn 19:27). This statement certainly means that the role of son was attributed to the disciple and that he assumed responsibility for the Mother of his beloved Master. And since Mary was given as a mother to him personally, the statement indicates, even though indirectly, everything expressed by the intimate relationship of a child with its mother. And all of this can be included in the word "entrusting." Such entrusting is *the response* to a person's love, and in particular *to the love of a mother*.

The Marian dimension of the life of a disciple of Christ is expressed in a special way precisely through this filial entrusting to the Mother of Christ, which began with the testament of the Redeemer on Golgotha. Entrusting himself to Mary in a filial manner, the Christian, like the Apostle John, "welcomes" the Mother of Christ "into his own home"[130] and brings her into everything that makes up his inner life, that is to say into his human and Christian "I": he *"took her to his own home."* Thus the Christian seeks to be taken into that "maternal charity" with which the Redeemer's Mother "cares for the brethren of her Son,"[131] "in whose birth and development she cooperates"[132] in the measure of the gift proper to each one through the power of Christ's Spirit. Thus also is exercised that motherhood in the Spirit which became Mary's role at the foot of the cross and in the upper room.

46. This filial relationship, this self-entrusting of a child to its mother, not only has its *beginning in Christ* but can also be said to be *definitively directed toward him.* Mary can be said to continue to say to each individual the words which she spoke at Cana in Galilee: "Do whatever he tells you." For he, Christ, is the one Mediator between God and mankind; he is "the way, and the truth, and the life" (Jn 14:6); it is he whom the Father has given to the world, so that man "should not perish but have eternal life" (Jn 3:16). The Virgin of Nazareth became the first "witness" of this saving love of the Father, and she also wishes *to remain* its *humble handmaid always and everywhere.* For every Christian, for every human being, Mary is the one who first "believed," and precisely with her faith as Spouse and Mother she wishes to act upon all those who entrust themselves to her as her children. And it is well known that the more her children persevere and progress in this attitude, the nearer Mary leads them to the "unsearchable riches of Christ" (Eph 3:8). And to the same degree they recognize more and more clearly the dignity of man in all its fullness and the definitive meaning of his vocation, for "Christ ... fully reveals man to man himself."[133]

This Marian dimension of Christian life takes on special importance in relation to women and their status. In fact, femininity has a *unique relationship* with the Mother of the

Redeemer, a subject which can be studied in greater depth elsewhere. Here I simply wish to note that the figure of Mary of Nazareth sheds light on *womanhood as such* by the very fact that God, in the sublime event of the Incarnation of his Son, entrusted himself to the ministry, the free and active ministry, of a woman. It can thus be said that women, by looking to Mary, find in her the secret of living their femininity with dignity and of achieving their own true advancement. In the light of Mary, the Church sees in the face of women the reflection of a beauty which mirrors the loftiest sentiments of which the human heart is capable: the self-offering totality of love; the strength that is capable of bearing the greatest sorrows; limitless fidelity and tireless devotion to work; the ability to combine penetrating intuition with words of support and encouragement.

47. At the Council Paul VI solemnly proclaimed that *Mary is the Mother of the Church*, "that is, Mother of the entire Christian people, both faithful and pastors."[134] Later, in 1968, in the profession of faith known as the "Credo of the People of God," he restated this truth in an even more forceful way in these words: "We believe that the Most Holy Mother of God, the new Eve, the Mother of the Church, carries on in heaven her maternal role with regard to the members of Christ, cooperating in the birth and development of divine life in the souls of the redeemed."[135]

The Council's teaching emphasized that the truth concerning the Blessed Virgin, Mother of Christ, is an effective aid in exploring more deeply the truth concerning the Church. When speaking of the Constitution *Lumen Gentium,* which had just been approved by the Council, Paul VI said: "Knowledge of the true Catholic doctrine regarding the Blessed Virgin Mary will always be a key to *the exact understanding of the mystery of Christ and of the Church.*"[136] Mary is present in the Church as the Mother of Christ, and at the same time as that Mother whom Christ, in the mystery of the redemption, gave to humanity in the person of the Apostle John. Thus, in her new motherhood in the Spirit, Mary embraces each and every one *in* the Church, and embraces each and every one *through* the Church. In this sense Mary, Mother of the Church, is also the Church's model. Indeed, as Paul VI hopes and asks, the Church must draw "from the Virgin Mother of God the most authentic form of perfect imitation of Christ."[137]

Thanks to this special bond linking the Mother of Christ with the Church, there is further *clarified the mystery of that "woman"* who, from the first chapters of the *Book of Genesis* until the Book of *Revelation,* accompanies the revelation of God's salvific plan for humanity. For Mary, present in the Church as the Mother of the Redeemer, takes part, as a mother, in that "monumental struggle against the powers of darkness"[138] which continues throughout human history. And by her ecclesial identification as the "woman clothed with the sun" (Rev 12:1),[139] it can be said that "in the most Holy Virgin the Church has already reached that perfection whereby she exists without spot or wrinkle." Hence, as Christians raise their eyes with faith to Mary in the course of their earthly pilgrimage, they "strive to increase in holiness."[140] Mary, the exalted Daughter of Zion, helps all her children, wherever they may be and whatever their condition, *to find in Christ the path to the Father's house.*

Thus, throughout her life, the Church maintains with the Mother of God a link which embraces, in the saving mystery, the past, the present, and the future, and venerates her as the spiritual mother of humanity and the advocate of grace.

The meaning of the Marian Year

48. It is precisely the special bond between humanity and this Mother that has led me to proclaim a Marian Year in the Church, in this period before the end of the second millennium since Christ's birth. A similar initiative was taken in the past, when Pius XII proclaimed 1954 as a Marian Year, in order to highlight the exceptional holiness of the Mother of Christ as expressed in the mysteries of her Immaculate Conception (defined exactly a century before) and of her Assumption into heaven.[141]

Now, following the line of the Second Vatican Council, I wish to emphasize the *special presence* of the Mother of God in the mystery of Christ and his Church. For this is a fundamental dimension emerging from the Mariology of the Council, the end of which is now more than twenty years behind us. The Extraordinary Synod of Bishops held in 1985 exhorted everyone to follow faithfully the teaching and guidelines of the Council. We can say that these two events —the Council and the synod—embody what the Holy Spirit himself wishes "to say to the Church" in the present phase of history.

In this context, the Marian Year is meant to promote a new and more careful reading of what the Council said about the Blessed Virgin Mary, Mother of God, in the mystery of Christ and of the Church, the topic to which the contents of this encyclical are devoted. Here we speak not only of the *doctrine of faith* but also of the *life of faith,* and thus of authentic "Marian spirituality," seen in the light of Tradition, and especially the spirituality to which the Council exhorts us.[142] Furthermore, Marian *spirituality,* like its corresponding *devotion,* finds a very rich source in the historical experience of individuals and of the various Christian communities present among the different peoples and nations of the world. In this regard, I would like to recall, among the many witnesses and teachers of this spirituality, the figure of St. Louis Marie Grignion de Montfort,[143] who proposes consecration to Christ through the hands of Mary, as an effective means for Christians to live faithfully their baptismal commitments. I am pleased to note that in our own time too new manifestations of this spirituality and devotion are not lacking.

There thus exist solid points of reference to look to and follow in the context of this Marian Year.

49. This Marian Year *will begin on the Solemnity of Pentecost, on June 7 next.* For it is a question not only of recalling that Mary "preceded" the entry of Christ the Lord into the history of the human family, but also of emphasizing, in the light of Mary, that from the moment when the mystery of the Incarnation was accomplished, human history entered "the fullness of time," and that the Church is the sign of this fullness. As the People of God, the Church

makes her pilgrim way toward eternity through faith, in the midst of all the peoples and nations, beginning from the day of Pentecost. *Christ's Mother*—who was present at the beginning of "the time of the Church," when in expectation of the coming of the Holy Spirit she devoted herself to prayer in the midst of the apostles and her Son's disciples—constantly "precedes" *the Church* in her *journey* through human history. She is also the one who, precisely as the "handmaid of the Lord," cooperates unceasingly with the work of salvation accomplished by Christ, her Son.

Thus by means of this Marian Year *the Church is called* not only to remember everything in her past that testifies to the special maternal cooperation of the Mother of God in the work of salvation in Christ the Lord, but also, on her own part, *to prepare* for the future the paths of this cooperation. For the end of the second Christian millennium opens up as a new prospect.

50. As has already been mentioned, also among our divided brethren many honor and celebrate the Mother of the Lord, especially among the Orientals. It is a Marian light cast upon ecumenism. In particular, I wish to mention once more that during the Marian Year there will occur the *millennium of the Baptism* of St. Vladimir, Grand Duke of Kiev (988). This marked the beginning of Christianity in the territories of what was then called Rus', and subsequently in other territories of Eastern Europe. In this way, through the work of evangelization, Christianity spread beyond Europe, as far as the northern territories of the Asian continent. We would therefore like, especially during this year, to join in prayer with

all those who are celebrating the millennium of this Baptism, both Orthodox and Catholics, repeating and confirming with the Council those sentiments of joy and comfort that "the Easterners . . . with ardent emotion and devout mind concur in reverencing the Mother of God, ever Virgin."[144] Even though we are still experiencing the painful effects of the separation which took place some decades later (1054), we can say that *in the presence of the Mother of Christ we feel that we are true brothers and sisters* within that messianic People, which is called to be the one family of God on earth. As I announced at the beginning of the New Year, "We desire to reconfirm this universal inheritance of all the sons and daughters of this earth."[145]

In announcing the Year of Mary, I also indicated that it will end next year on the *Solemnity of the Assumption of the Blessed Virgin into heaven,* in order to emphasize the "great sign in heaven" spoken of by the *Apocalypse.* In this way we also wish to respond to the exhortation of the Council, which looks to Mary as "a sign of sure hope and solace for the pilgrim People of God." And the Council expresses this exhortation in the following words: "Let the entire body of the faithful pour forth persevering prayer to the Mother of God and Mother of mankind. Let them implore that she who aided the beginning of the Church by her prayers may now, exalted as she is in heaven above all the saints and angels, intercede with her Son in the fellowship of all the saints. May she do so until all the peoples of the human family, whether they are honored with the name of Christian or whether they still do not know their Savior, are happily gathered together in peace and harmony into the one People of God, for the glory of the Most Holy and Undivided Trinity."[146]

PONDER

Churches split over the word *mediation*. Paul teaches that we would never be able to know God without Christ Jesus (par. 38). Jesus tells us the same in John 17. Both Paul and John are nonetheless *mediators*. Did either one of these writers hear these words from Jesus directly, or did someone tell them? Will we ever know?

The Church and all the churches are nothing but sheer mediation over and over again. A mother teaching a prayer, a father with hymnal in hand are mediators of the wonderful messages of the Redeemer. The very words on this page mediate. And what is it that we ultimately want to pass on with the Gospel message? There is a God who loves us and calls us into existence in order to come home to eternal love.

Today we rely on DNA to know our birth origins, but will a child really ever know if she was conceived as an act of love—or not? Only a parent, or the mediator of those parents, can tell us that part of the story.

So Mary needs to teach us about the love that brought this wondrous Son to us! We listen to her story, we look at her faithful love, we trust her, and we are amazed and happy. Was there ever a greater love story? Her destiny is eternally interwoven with his (par. 41) and at the same time with ours.

1. The Church speaks of four Marian dogmas, four teachings we are taught as unquestionably true about Mary: her motherhood, her virginity, her election in grace (Immaculate Conception), and her Assumption. John Paul II presents these teachings in the light of mediation. They speak to us of the intervention between God and his chosen creature, and these realities become gifts for us. But can we trust that these gifts of Mary are fruits that will also transform us in some way?

2. Both the Church and Mary are called Virgin and Mother. How can this be relevant to you? (par. 43)

3. We read, "The Redeemer entrusts his mother to the disciple, and at the same time he gives her to him as his mother. Mary's motherhood, which becomes man's inheritance, is a gift: *a gift which Christ himself makes* personally to every individual" (par. 45). If Christ gives the gift, have I accepted it? If so, how?

4. "He took her to his own home" (Jn 19:27). Have I? Has my parish?

PRAY

Mary, reading about you, thinking about you, and wondering, wondering, wondering, is different than attempting to speak to you. In church the other day, I saw someone going from statue to statue as if to say hello at each place. It struck me as odd. But it was different at your statue of the Sorrowful Mother. The person knelt there, gesturing with his hands, blowing his nose, and wiping away tears. I didn't want to look too intently. Then a time of quiet ensued. When he left, I wondered if you had responded in some way to bring peace to his obviously distressed situation. I hope so!

That experience stayed with me all day, dear Blessed Mother. It's hard to see a man so pained, pleading on his knees like that. Then I thought of your mediation, your listening ear, your open heart. I also realized that I had been thinking about this stranger and praying for him. That too is mediation.

Mary, please keep me attentive to the silent prayers of others. Help me to not judge on the basis of outward events, but to always search for the why, and to pray to know how our Father in heaven would want me to respond, even if it is just a quiet prayer in the midst of a busy life.

Act

Put away all your "crutches" today—whatever hinders you from believing in and trusting Mary's active presence among us—and talk to her. Speak with her about the mysterious ways of her Son. But remember to listen deeply for her response.

Conclusion

The wonder of Mary's divine motherhood

51. At the end of the daily Liturgy of the Hours, among the invocations addressed to Mary by the Church is the following:

"Loving Mother of the Redeemer,
gate of heaven, star of the sea,
assist your people who have fallen yet strive to rise again.
To the wonderment of nature you bore your Creator!"

"To the wonderment of nature"! These words of the antiphon express that *wonderment of faith* which accompanies the mystery of Mary's divine motherhood. In a sense, it does so in the heart of the whole of creation, and, directly, in the heart of the whole People of God, in the heart of the Church. How wonderfully far God has gone, the Creator and Lord of all things, in the "revelation of himself" to man![147] How clearly he has bridged all the spaces of that infinite "distance" which separates the Creator from the creature! If in himself he remains *ineffable and unsearchable,* still more *ineffable and unsearchable is he in the reality of the Incarnation* of the Word, who became man through the Virgin of Nazareth.

If he has eternally willed to call man to share in the divine nature (cf. 2 Pt 1:4), it can be said that he has matched the "divinization" of man to humanity's historical conditions, so that even after sin he is ready to restore at a great price the eternal plan of his love through the "humanization" of his Son, who is of the same being as himself. The whole of creation, and more directly man himself, cannot fail to be amazed at this gift in which he has become a sharer, in the Holy Spirit: "God so loved the world that he gave his only Son" (Jn 3:16).

At the center of this mystery, in the midst of this wonderment of faith, stands Mary. As the loving Mother of the Redeemer, she was the first to experience it: "To the wonderment of nature you bore your Creator"!

Mary and the transformation of humanity

52. The words of this liturgical antiphon also express *the truth of the "great transformation"* which the mystery of the Incarnation establishes for man. It is a transformation which belongs to his entire history, from that beginning which is revealed to us in the first chapters of *Genesis* until the final end, in the perspective of the end of the world, of which Jesus has revealed to us "neither the day nor the hour" (Mt 25:13). It is an unending and continuous transformation between falling and rising again, between the man of sin and the man of grace and justice. The Advent liturgy in particular is at the very heart of this transformation and captures its unceasing "here and now" when it exclaims: "Assist your people who have fallen yet strive to rise again"!

These words apply to every individual, every community, to nations and peoples, and to the generations and epochs of human history, to our own epoch, to these years of the millennium which is drawing to a close: "Assist, yes assist, your people who have fallen"!

This is the invocation addressed to Mary, the "loving Mother of the Redeemer," the invocation addressed to Christ, who through Mary entered human history. Year after year the antiphon rises to Mary, evoking that moment which saw the accomplishment of this essential historical transformation, which irreversibly continues: the transformation from "falling" to "rising."

Mankind has made wonderful discoveries and achieved extraordinary results in the fields of science and technology. It has made great advances along the path of progress and civilization, and in recent times one could say that it has succeeded in speeding up the pace of history. But the fundamental transformation, the one which can be called "original," constantly accompanies man's journey, and through all the events of history accompanies each and every individual. It is the transformation from "falling" to "rising," from death to life. It is also *a constant challenge* to people's consciences, a challenge to man's whole historical awareness: the challenge to follow the path of "not falling" in ways that are ever old and ever new, and of "rising again" if a fall has occurred.

As she goes forward with the whole of humanity toward the frontier between the two millennia, the Church, for her part, with the whole community of believers and in union with all men and women of good will, takes up the great challenge contained in these words of the Marian antiphon: "the people who have fallen yet strive to rise again," and she addresses both the Redeemer and his Mother with the plea: "Assist us." For as this prayer attests, the Church sees the Blessed Mother of God in the saving mystery of Christ and in her own mystery. She sees Mary deeply rooted in humanity's history, in man's eternal vocation according to the providential plan which God has made for him from eternity. She sees Mary maternally present and sharing in the many complicated problems which *today* beset the lives of individuals, families, and nations; she sees her helping the Christian people in the constant struggle between good and evil, to ensure that it "does not fall," or, if it has fallen, that it "rises again."

I hope with all my heart that the reflections contained in the present encyclical will also serve to renew this vision in the hearts of all believers.

As Bishop of Rome, I send to all those to whom these thoughts are addressed the kiss of peace, my greeting, and my blessing in our Lord Jesus Christ. Amen.

Given in Rome, at St. Peter's, on March 25, the Solemnity of the Annunciation of the Lord, in the year 1987, the ninth of my pontificate.

Joannes Paulus pp. II

Notes

1. Cf. Second Vatican Ecumenical Council, Dogmatic Constitution on the Church *Lumen Gentium,* 52 and the whole of Chapter VIII, entitled "The Role of the Blessed Virgin Mary, Mother of God, in the Mystery of Christ and the Church."

2. The expression "fullness of time" *(pléroma tou chrónou)* is parallel with similar expressions of Judaism, both Biblical (cf. Gen 29:21; 1 Sam 7:12; Tob 14:5) and extra-Biblical, and especially of the New Testament (cf. Mk 1:15; Lk 21:24; Jn 7:8; Eph 1:10). From the point of view of form, it means not only the conclusion of a chronological process but also and especially the coming to maturity or completion of a particularly important period, one directed toward the fulfillment of an expectation, a coming to completion which thus takes on an eschatological dimension. According to Galatians 4:4 and its context, it is the coming of the Son of God that reveals that time has, so to speak, reached its limit. That is to say, the period marked by the promise made to Abraham and by the Law mediated by Moses has now reached its climax, in the sense that Christ fulfills the divine promise and supersedes the old Law.

3. Cf. *Roman Missal,* Preface of December 8, Immaculate Conception of the Blessed Virgin Mary; St. Ambrose, *De Institutione Virginis,* XV, 93–94: *PL* 16, 342; Dogmatic Constitution on the Church *Lumen Gentium,* 68.

4. Dogmatic Constitution on the Church *Lumen Gentium,* 58.

5. Pope Paul VI, Encyclical Epistle *Christi Matri* (September 15, 1966): *AAS* 58 (1966), 745–749; Apostolic Exhortation *Signum Magnum*

(May 13, 1967): *AAS* 59 (1967), 465–475; Apostolic Exhortation *Marialis Cultus* (February 2, 1974): *AAS* 66 (1974), 113–168.

6. The Old Testament foretold in many different ways the mystery of Mary: cf. St. John Damascene, *Hom. in Dormitionem* 1, 8–9: *SCh* 80, 103–107.

7. Cf. *Insegnamenti di Giovanni Paolo II*, VI/2 (1983), 225–226; Pope Pius IX, Apostolic Letter *Ineffabilis Deus* (December 8, 1854): *Pius IX P. M. Acta*, I, 597–599.

8. Cf. Pastoral Constitution on the Church in the Modern World *Gaudium et Spes*, 22.

9. Ecumenical Council of Ephesus, in *Conciliorum Oecumenicorum Decreta*, Bologna 1973, 41–44, 59–61: *DS* 250–264; cf. Ecumenical Council of Chalcedon, *op. cit.* 84–87: *DS* 300–303.

10. Pastoral Constitution on the Church in the Modern World *Gaudium et Spes*, 22.

11. Dogmatic Constitution on the Church *Lumen Gentium*, 52.

12. Cf. ibid., 58.

13. Ibid., 63, cf. St. Ambrose, *Expos. Evang. sec. Lucam*, II, 7: *CSEL* 32/4, 45; *De Institutione Virginis*, XIV, 88–89: *PL* 16, 341.

14. Cf. Dogmatic Constitution on the Church *Lumen Gentium*, 64.

15. Ibid., 65.

16. "Take away this star of the sun which illuminates the world: where does the day go? Take away Mary, this star of the sea, of the great and boundless sea: what is left but a vast obscurity and the shadow of death and deepest darkness?": St. Bernard, *In Navitate Beatae Mariae Sermo, De Aquaeductu*, 6: *Sancti Bernardi Opera*, V, 1968, 279; cf. *In Laudibus Virginis Matris Homilia* II, 17: *loc. cit.*, IV, 1966, 34–35.

17. Dogmatic Constitution on the Church *Lumen Gentium*, 63.

18. Ibid., 63.

19. Concerning the predestination of Mary, cf. St. John Damascene, *Hom. in Nativitatem*, 7, 10: *SCh* 80, 65; 73; *Hom. in Dormitionem* 1, 3: *SCh* 80, 85: "For it is she, who, chosen from the ancient generations, by

virtue of the predestination and benevolence of the God and Father who generated you (the Word of God) outside time without coming out of himself or suffering change, it is she who gave you birth, nourished of her flesh, in the last time. . . ."

20. Dogmatic Constitution on the Church *Lumen Gentium*, 55.

21. In Patristic tradition there is a wide and varied interpretation of this expression: cf. Origen, *In Lucam homiliae*, VI, 7: *SCh* 87, 148; Severianus of Gabala, *In Mundi Creationem, Oratio* VI, 10: *PG* 56, 497f.; St. John Chrysostom (Pseudo), *In Annuntiationem Deiparae et contra Arium impium, PG* 62, 765f.; Basil of Seleucia, *Oratio* 39, *In Sanctissimae Deiparae Annuntiationem*, 5: *PG* 85, 441–46; Antipater of Bosra, *Hom. II, In Sanctissimae Deiparae Annuntiationem*, 3–11: *PG* 85, 1777–1783; St. Sophronius of Jerusalem, *Oratio 11, In Sanctissimae Deiparae Annuntiationem*, 17–19: *PG* 87/3, 3235–3240; St. John Damascene *Hom. in Dormitionem*, 1, 70: *SCh* 80, 96–101; St. Jerome, *Epistola* 65, 9: *PL* 22, 628; St. Ambrose, *Expos. Evang. sec. Lucam*, II, 9: *CSEL* 32/4, 45f.; St. Augustine, *Sermo* 291, 4–6: *PL* 38, 1318–1319; *Enchiridion*, 36, 11: *PL* 40, 250; St. Peter Chrysologus, *Sermo* 142: *PL* 52, 579–580; *Sermo* 143: *PL* 52, 583; St. Fulgentius of Ruspe, *Epistola* 17, VI, 12: *PL* 65, 458; St. Bernard, *In Laudibus Virginis Matris, Homilia* III, 2–3: *Sancti Bernardi Opera, IV,* 1966, 36–38.

22. Dogmatic Constitution on the Church *Lumen Gentium*, 55.

23. Ibid., 53.

24. Cf. Pope Pius IX, Apostolic Letter *Ineffabilis Deus* (December 8, 1854): *Pius IX P. M. Acta,* I, 616; Dogmatic Constitution on the Church *Lumen Gentium*, 53.

25. Cf. St. Germanus of Constantinople, *In Annuntiationem SS. Deiparae Hom.: PG* 98, 327–328; St. Andrew of Crete, *Canon in B. Mariae Natalem,* 4: *PG* 97, 1321–1322, *In Nativitatem B. Mariae,* I: *PG* 97, 811–812; *Hom. in Dormitionem S. Mariae* I: *PG* 97, 1067–1068.

26. *Liturgy of the Hours* of August 15, Assumption of the Blessed Virgin Mary, Hymn at First and Second Vespers; St. Peter Damian, *Carmina et Preces,* 47: *PL* 145, 934.

27. *The Divine Comedy,* Paradise, XXXIII, 1; cf. *Liturgy of the Hours,* Memorial of the Blessed Virgin Mary on Saturday, Hymn II in the Office of Readings.

28. Cf. St. Augustine, *De Sancta Virginitate,* III, 3: *PL* 40, 398; *Sermo* 25, 7: *PL* 46,

29. Dogmatic Constitution on Divine Revelation *Dei Verbum,* 5

30. This is a classic theme, already expounded by St. Irenaeus: "And, as by the action of the disobedient virgin, man was afflicted and, being cast down, died, so also by the action of the Virgin who obeyed the Word of God, man being regenerated received, through life, life. . . . For it was meet and just . . . that Eve should be "recapitulated" in Mary, so that the Virgin, becoming the advocate of the virgin, should dissolve and destroy the virginal disobedience by means of virginal obedience": *Expositio Doctrinae Apostolicae,* 33: *SCh* 62, 83–86; cf. also *Adversus Haereses,* V, 19, 1: *SCh* 153, 248–250.

31. Dogmatic Constitution on Divine Revelation *Dei Verbum,* 5.

32. Ibid., 5; cf. Dogmatic Constitution on the Church *Lumen Gentium,* 56.

33. Dogmatic Constitution on the Church *Lumen Gentium,* 56.

34. Ibid., 56.

35. Cf. ibid., 53; St. Augustine, *De Sancta Virginitate,* III, 3: *PL* 40, 398; *Sermo* 215, 4; *PL* 38, 1074; *Sermo* 196, 1: *PL* 38, 1019; *De peccatorum meritis et remissione,* I, 29, 57: *PL* 44, 142; *Sermo* 25, 7: *PL* 46, 937–938; St. Leo the Great, *Tractatus* 21, *De Natale Domini,* I: *CCL* 138, 86.

36. *Ascent of Mount Carmel,* Book II, Ch. 3, 4–6.

37. Cf. Dogmatic Constitution on the Church *Lumen Gentium,* 58.

38. Ibid., 58.

39. Cf. Dogmatic Constitution on Divine Revelation *Dei Verbum,* 5.

40. Concerning Mary's participation or "compassion" in the death of Christ, cf. St. Bernard, In Dominica infra octavam Assumptionis Sermo, 14: Sancti Bernardi Opera, V, 1968, 273.

41. St. Irenaeus, *Adversus Haereses*, III, 22, 4: *SCh* 211, 438–444; cf. Dogmatic Constitution on the Church *Lumen Gentium*, 56, note 6.

42. Cf. Dogmatic Constitution on the Church *Lumen Gentium*, 56, and the Fathers quoted there in notes 8 and 9.

43. "Christ is truth, Christ is flesh: Christ truth in the mind of Mary, Christ flesh in the womb of Mary": St. Augustine, *Sermo* 25 *(Sermones inediti)*, 7: *PL* 46, 938.

44. Dogmatic Constitution on the Church *Lumen Gentium*, 60.

45. Ibid., 61.

46. Ibid., 62.

47. There is a well known passage of Origen on the presence of Mary and John on Calvary: "The Gospels are the first fruits of all Scripture and the Gospel of John is the first of the Gospels: no one can grasp its meaning without having leaned his head on Jesus' breast and having received from Jesus, Mary as Mother": *Comm. in Ioan.*, I, 6: *PG* 14, 31; cf. St. Ambrose, *Expos. Evang. sec. Lucam*, X, 129–131: *CSEL* 32/4, 504f.

48. Dogmatic Constitution on the Church *Lumen Gentium*, 54 and 53; the latter text quotes St. Augustine, *De Sancta Virginitate*, VI, 6: *PL* 40, 399.

49. Dogmatic Constitution on the Church *Lumen Gentium*, 55.

50. Cf. St. Leo the Great, *Tractatus* 26, *De Natale Domini*, 2: *CCL* 138, 126.

51. Dogmatic Constitution on the Church *Lumen Gentium*, 59.

52. St. Augustine, *De Civitate Dei*, XVIII, 51: *CCL* 48, 650.

53. Dogmatic Constitution on the Church *Lumen Gentium*, 8.

54. Ibid., 9.

55. Ibid., 9.

56. Ibid., 8.

57. Ibid., 9.

58. Ibid., 65.

59. Ibid., 59.

60. Cf. Dogmatic Constitution on Divine Revelation *Dei Verbum,* 5.

61. Cf. Dogmatic Constitution on the Church *Lumen Gentium,* 63.

62. Cf. ibid., 9.

63. Cf. ibid., 65.

64. Ibid., 65.

65. Ibid., 65.

66. Cf. ibid., 13.

67. Cf. ibid., 13.

68. Cf. ibid., 13.

69. Cf. *Roman Missal,* formula of the consecration of the chalice in the Eucharistic Prayers.

70. Dogmatic Constitution on the Church *Lumen Gentium,* 1.

71. Ibid., 13.

72. Ibid., 15.

73. Cf. Second Vatican Ecumenical Council, Decree on Ecumenism *Unitatis Redintegratio,* 1.

74. Dogmatic Constitution on the Church *Lumen Gentium,* 68, 69. On Mary Most Holy, promoter of Christian unity, and on the cult of Mary in the East, cf. Leo XIII, Encyclical Epistle *Adiutricem Populi* (September 5, 1895): *Acta Leonis,* XV, 300–312.

75. Cf. Decree on Ecumenism *Unitatis Redintegratio,* 20.

76. Cf. ibid., 19.

77. Ibid., 14.

78. Ibid., 15.

79. Dogmatic Constitution on the Church *Lumen Gentium,* 66.

80. Ecumenical Council of Chalcedon, *Definitio fidei: Conciliorum Oecumenicorum Decreta,* Bologna, 1973, 86 (*DS* 301).

81. Cf. *the Weddase Maryam* (Praises of Mary), which follows the Ethiopian Psalter and contains hymns and prayers to Mary for each day of the week. Cf. also the *Matshafa Kidana Mehrat (Book of the Pact of Mercy);* the importance given to Mary in the Ethiopian hymnology and liturgy deserves to be emphasized.

82. Cf. St. Ephrem, *Hymni de Nativitate: Scriptores Syri,* 82, *CSCO,* 186.

83. Cf. St. Gregory of Narek, *Le livre de prières: SCh* 78, 160–163, 428–432.

84. Second Ecumenical Council of Nicaea: *Conciliorum Oecumenicorum Decreta,* Bologna, 1973, 135–138 (*DS* 600–609).

85. Cf. Dogmatic Constitution on the Church *Lumen Gentium,* 59.

86. Cf. Decree on Ecumenism *Unitatis Redintegratio,* 19.

87. Dogmatic Constitution on the Church *Lumen Gentium,* 8.

88. Ibid., 9.

89. As is well known, the words of the *Magnificat* contain or echo numerous passages of the Old Testament.

90. Dogmatic Constitution on Divine Revelation *Dei Verbum,* 2.

91. Cf., for example, St. Justin, *Dialogus cum Tryphone Iudaeo,* 100: Otto II, 358; St. Irenaeus, *Adversus Haereses* III, 22, 4: *SCh* 211, 439–445; Tertullian, *De Carne Christi,* 17, 4–6: *CCL* 2, 904–905.

92. Cf. St. Epiphanius, *Panarion,* III, 2; *Haer.* 78, 18: *PG* 42, 727–730.

93. Congregation for the Doctrine of the Faith, *Instruction on Christian Freedom and Liberation* (March 22, 1986), 97.

94. Dogmatic Constitution on the Church *Lumen Gentium,* 60.

95. Ibid., 60.

96. Cf. the formula of mediatrix *"ad Mediatorem"* of St. Bernard, *In Dominica infra octavam Assumptionis Sermo,* 2: *Sancti Bernardi Opera,* V, 1968, 263. Mary as a pure mirror sends back to her Son all the glory and honor which she receives: St. Bernard, *In Nativitate Beatae Mariae Sermo, De Aquaeductu,* 12: *loc. cit.,* 283.

97. Dogmatic Constitution on the Church *Lumen Gentium,* 62.

98. Ibid., 62.

99. Ibid., 61.

100. Ibid., 62.

101. Ibid., 61.

102. Ibid., 61.

103. Ibid., 62.

104. Ibid., 62.

105. Ibid., 62; in her prayer too the Church recognizes and celebrates Mary's "maternal role": it is a role "of intercession and forgiveness, petition and grace, reconciliation and peace" (cf. Preface of the Mass of the Blessed Virgin Mary, Mother and Mediatrix of Grace, in *Collectio Missarum de Beata Maria Virgine, editio typica* 1987, I, 120).

106. Ibid., 62.

107. Ibid., 62; cf. St. John Damascene, *Hom. in Dormitionem,* I, 11; II, 2, 14; III, 2: *SCh* 80, 111–112; 127–131; 157–161; 181–185; St. Bernard, *In Assumptione Beatae Mariae Sermo,* 1–2: *Sancti Bernardi Opera,* V, 1968, 228–238.

108. Dogmatic Constitution on the Church *Lumen Gentium,* 59; cf. Pope Pius XII, Apostolic Constitution *Munificentissimus Deus* (November 1, 1950): *AAS* 42 (1950) 769–771; St. Bernard presents Mary immersed in the splendor of the Son's glory: In *Dominica Infra Octavam Assumptionis Sermo,* 3; *Sancti Bernardi Opera,* V, 1968, 263–264.

109. Dogmatic Constitution on the Church *Lumen Gentium,* 53.

110. On this particular aspect of Mary's mediation as *implorer of clemency* from the "Son as Judge," cf. St. Bernard, *In Dominica infra octavam Assumptionis Sermo,* 1–2: *Sancti Bernardi Opera,* V, 1968, 262–263; Pope Leo XIII, Encyclical Epistle *Octobri Mense* (September 22, 1891): *Leonis XIII P. M. Acta,* XI, 299–315.

111. Dogmatic Constitution on the Church *Lumen Gentium,* 55.

112. Ibid., 59.

113. Ibid., 36.

114. Ibid., 36.

115. With regard to Mary as Queen, cf. St. John Damascene, *Hom. in Nativitatem,* 6; 12; *Hom. in Dormitionem,* 1, 2, 12, 14; II, 11; III, 4: *SCh* 80, 59–60, 77–78, 83–84, 113–114, 117, 151–152, 189–193.

116. Dogmatic Constitution on the Church *Lumen Gentium*, 62.

117. Ibid., 63.

118. Ibid., 63.

119. Ibid., 66.

120. Cf. St. Ambrose, *De Institutione Virginis*, XIV, 88–89: *PL* 16, 341, St. Augustine, *Sermo* 215, 4: *PL* 38, 1074; *De Sancta Virginitate*, II, 2; V, 5; VI, 6: *PL* 40, 397, 398–399; *Sermo* 191, II, 3: *PL* 38, 1010–1011.

121. Cf. Dogmatic Constitution on the Church *Lumen Gentium*, 63

122. Ibid., 64.

123. Ibid., 64.

124. Ibid., 64.

125. Ibid., 64.

126. Cf. Dogmatic Constitution on Divine Revelation *Dei Verbum*, 8; St. Bonaventure, *Comment. in Evang. Lucae, Ad Claras Aquas*, VII, 53, no. 40, 68, no. 109.

127. Dogmatic Constitution on the Church *Lumen Gentium*, 64.

128. Ibid., 63.

129. Cf. ibid., 63.

130. Clearly, in the Greek text the expression *"eis ta idia"* goes beyond the mere acceptance of Mary by the disciple in the sense of material lodging and hospitality in his house; it indicates rather a *communion of life* established between the two as a result of the words of the dying Christ: cf. St. Augustine, *In Ioan. Evang. Tract.*, 119, 3: *CCL* 36, 659: "He took her to himself, not into his own property, for he possessed nothing of his own, but among his own duties, which he attended to with dedication."

131. Dogmatic Constitution on the Church *Lumen Gentium*, 62.

132. Ibid., 63.

133. Pastoral Constitution on the Church in the Modern World *Gaudium et Spes*, 22.

134. Cf. Pope Paul VI, , *Address at the Closing of the Third Session of the Second Vatican Ecumenical Council* (November 21, 1964): *AAS* 56 (1964), 1015.

135. Pope Paul VI, *Solemn Profession of Faith* (June 30, 1968), 15: *AAS* 60 (1968), 438f.

136. Pope Paul VI, *Address, op. cit.,* 1015.

137. Ibid., 1016.

138. Cf. Pastoral Constitution on the Church in the Modern World *Gaudium et Spes,* 37.

139. Cf. St. Bernard, *In Dominica infra octavam Assumptionis Sermo: Sancti Bernardi Opera* V, 1968, 262–274.

140. Dogmatic Constitution on the Church *Lumen Gentium,* 65.

141. Cf. Encyclical Letter *Fulgens Corona* (September 8, 1953): *AAS* 45 (1953), 577–592. Pius X with his Encyclical Letter *Ad Diem Illum* (February 2, 1904), on the occasion of the 50th anniversary of the dogmatic definition of the Immaculate Conception of the Blessed Virgin Mary, had proclaimed an extraordinary jubilee of a few months; Pius X, *P. M. Acta,* I, 147–166.

142. Cf. Dogmatic Constitution on the Church *Lumen Gentium,* 66–67.

143. St. Louis Marie Grignion de Montfort, *True Devotion to the Blessed Virgin Mary.* This saint can rightly be linked with the figure of St. Alphonsus Liguori, the second centenary of whose death occurs this year; cf. among his works *The Glories of Mary.*

144. Dogmatic Constitution on the Church *Lumen Gentium,* 69.

145. Homily (January 1, 1987), 4: *AAS* 79 (1987), 1148.

146. Dogmatic Constitution on the Church *Lumen Gentium,* 69.

147. Cf. Dogmatic Constitution on Divine Revelation *Dei Verbum,* 2: "Through this revelation . . . the invisible God . . . out of the abundance of his love speaks to men as friends . . . and lives among them . . . so that he may invite and take them into fellowship with himself."

A member of the Secular Institute of the Schoenstatt Sisters of Mary, Jean Frisk holds a licentiate in sacred theology from the Marian Library / International Marian Research Institute. Her research explores how we teach about Mary, the Mother of Jesus in catechetical texts and media resources. She has authored award-winning texts on various aspects of Marian spirituality, is a textbook consultant, and teaches Marian catechesis at the International Marian Research Institute where she also oversees the maintenance of Marian art and a vast collection of nativities.

BOOKS & MEDIA

A mission of the Daughters of St. Paul

As apostles of Jesus Christ, evangelizing today's world:

We are CALLED to holiness
by God's living Word and Eucharist.

We COMMUNICATE the Gospel message
through our lives and through all
available forms of media.

We SERVE the Church
by responding to the hopes and needs
of all people with the Word of God,
in the spirit of St. Paul.

For more information visit our website: www.pauline.org.

BOOKS & MEDIA

The Daughters of St. Paul operate book and media centers at the following addresses. Visit, call or write the one nearest you today, or find us on the World Wide Web, www.pauline.org

CALIFORNIA

3908 Sepulveda Blvd, Culver City, CA 90230	310-397-8676
935 Brewster Avenue, Redwood City, CA 94063	650-369-4230
5945 Balboa Avenue, San Diego, CA 92111	858-565-9181

FLORIDA

145 S.W. 107th Avenue, Miami, FL 33174	305-559-6715

HAWAII

1143 Bishop Street, Honolulu, HI 96813	808-521-2731
Neighbor Islands call:	866-521-2731

ILLINOIS

172 North Michigan Avenue, Chicago, IL 60601	312-346-4228

LOUISIANA

4403 Veterans Memorial Blvd, Metairie, LA 70006	504-887-7631

MASSACHUSETTS

885 Providence Hwy, Dedham, MA 02026	781-326-5385

MISSOURI

9804 Watson Road, St. Louis, MO 63126	314-965-3512

NEW YORK

64 W. 38th Street, New York, NY 10018	212-754-1110

PENNSYLVANIA

Philadelphia—relocating	215-676-9494

SOUTH CAROLINA

243 King Street, Charleston, SC 29401	843-577-0175

VIRGINIA

1025 King Street, Alexandria, VA 22314	703-549-3806

CANADA

3022 Dufferin Street, Toronto, ON M6B 3T5	416-781-9131

¡También somos su fuente para libros,
videos y música en español!